Advanced Studies in Economic Sciences
Information Systems, Economics and OR

Advanced Studies in Economic Sciences
Information Systems, Economics and OR

Edited by
 Kazunori Morioka
 Atsushi Kadoya
 Hiroshima Shudo University

Volume 10 in a Series of Monographs of Contemporary Social Systems Solutions
 Produced by the Faculty of Economic Sciences, Hiroshima Shudo University

Kyushu University Press

Volume 10 in a Series of Monographs of Contemporary Social Systems Solutions
Produced by Hiroshima Shudo University

All rights reserved. No part of this publication may be reproduced or transmitted in any form or by any means, electronic or mechanical, including photocopying and recording, or by any information storage and retrieval system, without the written permission from the publisher.

Copyright © 2019 by Kazunori Morioka and Atsushi Kadoya
3-8-34-305, Momochihama, Sawara-ku, Fukuoka-shi, 814-0001, Japan

ISBN978-4-7985-0258-8

Printed in Japan

Preface

Hiroshima Shudo University established the Faculty of Economic Sciences in 1977 and the Graduate School of Economic Sciences in 2001. One goal of this faculty is to unify information sciences and economics and the faculty has endeavored to make progress in the research fields of operations research, computer sciences, mathematical economics and econometrics. While the definition of economic sciences has not been established yet, our specific understanding is that the economic sciences should unite system sciences and qualitative economic analysis and construct new fields relating to the management of the international economy, the financial system, and the national economy, or environmental issues, legal policies in communication.

The Faculty of Economic Sciences is a unique academic institution. There are no other faculties titled as "economic sciences" in Japan. Basically, we pursue analyzing various issues of contemporary economies and social systems, but its uniqueness can be observed in our efforts to balance the traditional economics and information sciences as means of analytical tools.

The Faculty consists of some 30 highly qualified members, whose research interests span a wide range of topics but more or less concern quantitative analytical frameworks. Since 2005 we have been publishing our research results in a form of monographs in English, one or two volumes a year, in order to present our academic contributions to possible readers in the world.

In the past several years, members of this faculty have made plans to expand these new frontiers as follows:

1. Macro-econometric models or micro-models which contain international economics or micro-models.
2. System analysis of financial institutions and international trade.
3. Information sciences, such as network systems or information systems or theory of reliance.
4. System sciences, such as operations research and production system analysis.
5. Research on information society and social systems.
6. Legal informatics, applying information technology to legal fields and solution of legal problems in digital society.
7. Environmental Economics, researching environmental issues from the economic viewpoints.

Faculty members have undertaken joint research with the aim of constructing these new fields and to publish our new research as a monograph as follows:

*Quantitative Economic Analysis, International Trade and Finance (2005)
*Applied Economic Informatics and Systems Sciences (2005)
*Quantitative Analysis of Modern Economy (2007)
*System Sciences for Economics and Informatics (2007)
*Quantitative Analysis on Contemporary Economic Issues (2008)
*Research on Information Society and Social Systems (2008)
*Social Systems Solutions by Legal Informatics, Economic Sciences and Computer Sciences (2009)
*The New Viewpoints and New Solutions of Economic Sciences in the Information Society (2010)
*Social Systems Solutions Applied by Economic Sciences and Mathematical Solutions (2011)
*Social Systems Solutions through Economic Sciences (2012)
*Legal Informatics, Economic Science and Mathematical Research (2013)
*New Solutions in Legal Informatics, Economic Sciences and Mathematics (2014)
*Contemporary Works in Economic Sciences: Legal Informatics, Economics, OR and Mathematics (2015)
* Challenging Researches in Economic Sciences : Legal Informatics, Environmental Economics, Economics, OR and Mathematics (2016)
*Recent Studies in Economic Sciences : Information Systems, Project Managements, Economics, OR and Mathematics (2017)

In these monographs our aim is to develop new methods and materials for constructing new fields of economics.

The authors of papers in these monographs have participate in building this new faculty and worked to develop new horizons of system sciences, information sciences, economics, economic sciences, environmental economics, computer sciences and legal informatics. We would welcome comments or suggestions in any forms.

The 2018 monograph is also entirely financed by the Faculty of Economic Sciences and is entitled under the title of "Advanced Studies in Economic Sciences : Information Systems, Economics and OR" edited by Kazunori Morioka and Atsushi Kadoya.

This book contains contributions from wide variety of research in information society, information sciences, environmental economics, economic sciences, systems approach to the economic, managerial, mathematical, environmental, and legal subjects. The focus of most articles is on the recent developments in the relevant. The set of papers in this book reflect both each theory and wide range of applications to economic and managerial models. The economic sciences is based upon an interdisciplinary education and research area of sciences economics, econometrics, statistics, information sciences, system sciences, application information sciences, operations research and legal informatics.

Preface

This book consists of five chapters as follows:

Chapter 1 is written by Chris Czerkawski and Osamu Kurihara. In this paper, the Authors use methodology developed by Corbae (1987) which is based on the cointegration model and allows the existence of stationarity and risk-free premium to test a condition for efficiency in selected time periods in the forward market. They will provide an introduction to the topic.

Chapter 2 is written by Nan Zhang and Li Zhu. This paper try to clarify global uncertainty from the view of global flow of funds by investigating the uncertain shocking influence of Cross-Border Financing between China, Japan, and the U.S. using the Bank for International Settlements Locational Banking Statistics data. The dyadic structure of this data allows to disentangle supply and demand factors and to better identify the effect of uncertainty shocks on cross-border banking flows.

Chapter 3 is written by Sithanonxay Suvannaphakdy and Toshihisa Toyoda. Trade liberalization entails the transition from trade taxes to domestic taxes. Certain structural characteristics such as narrow tax base and significant proportion of subsistence sectors, however, constrain such transition and hence reducing public revenues in developing countries. This paper contributes to this debate by assessing the impact of trade liberalization on domestic tax revenue in Laos. They find that Laos has been able to recover revenue loss from tariff reduction through the introduction of value-added tax.

Chapter 4 is written by Hiroyuki Dekihara. In this paper, the new spatial data structure is proposed by extending the MD-tree which is one of the efficient spatial data structures using an update algorithm for spatial data structures managing moving objects. It is called the BUMD (the Batch Update MD) -tree. The novel concepts of the BUMD-tree are a butch insertion using a buffer array, and a simplified restructuring according to the location changes of objects. The BUMD-tree saves the update cost of the tree by using the buffer array in which reported new locations of the moving objects are stored. Moreover, the search performances of the BUMD-tree are kept although the restructuring of the tree is not performed completely.

Chapter 5 is written by Setsuko Sakai and Tetsuyuki Takahama. In this paper, the equivalent penalty coefficient value (EPC) is proposed for population-based optimization algorithms (POAs). EPC can be defined in POAs where a new solution is compared with the old solution. EPC is the penalty coefficient value that makes the two extended objective values of the solutions the same. Search that gives priority to objective values is realized by selecting a small EPC in a population. Search that gives priority to constraint violations is realized by selecting a large EPC. It is expected that the adaptive control of the penalty coefficient can be realized by selecting an appropriate EPC. The proposed method is introduced to differential evolution. The nature of the proposed method is shown by solving several constrained optimization problems.

We hope that these articles provide a comprehensive yet lively and up-to-date discussion of the state-of-the-art in information society, social systems, and the relevant research fields. We believe that this book contains a coherent view of the important unifying ideas throughout the many faces of systems approach and a guide to the most significant current areas of approach.

We also appreciate that this book should contribute to build the ubiquitous society in Japan. We would like to thank Hiroshima Shudo University and the Faculty of Economic Sciences for financial supports of publishing this monograph. Also we would like to take the opportunity to thank Kyushu University Press for publishing this book and for authors for their contributions.

Finally, a profound thanks goes to our families, in continuing appreciation of their support and many other contributions.

November, 2018
Kazunori Morioka
Atsushi Kadoya

Contents

Preface i

Chapter 1 Testing the Efficiency of Foreign Exchange Market – Part1
.... *Chris Czerkawski and Osamu Kurihara* 1
  1. Introduction and Review of Literature 1
  2. Methodology 4

Chapter 2 Global Flow of Funds and Uncertainty:
         Focus on the Cross-Border Financing .... *Nan Zhang and Li Zhu* 11
  1. Introduction 11
  2. Statistical Framework and Global Flow of Funds Matrix 14
  3. Data Sources for Measuring Cross-Border Financing 20
  4. Econometric Model and Empirical Findings 21
  5. Conclusion 28

Chapter 3 Assessing the Fiscal Impact of Trade Liberalization in Laos:
         A General Equilibrium Approach
.... *Sithanonxay Suvannaphakdy and Toshihisa Toyoda* 33
  1. Introduction 34
  2. Background to the Lao Economy 35
  3. Transition from Tariff to Domestic Taxes in Laos 38
  4. CGE Modelling and Data 40
  5. Simulation Results and Policy Implications 43
  6. Conclusions 48

Chapter 4 BUMD-tree: An Extended MD-tree using Batch Update Algorithm
         for Management of Moving Objects .... *Hiroyuki Dekihara* 53
  1. Introduction 53
  2. Management of Moving Objects 54
  3. The BUMD-tree 56
  4. Experimental Results 60
  5. Conclusion 63

Chapter 5   A Study on an Equivalent Penalty Coefficient Value for Adaptive Control of the Penalty Coefficient in Constrained Optimization by Differential Evolution
.... *Setsuko Sakai and Tetsuyuki Takahama*   65
   1. Introduction 65
   2. Solving Constrained Optimization Problems 66
   3. Differential Evolution 67
   4. Proposed Method 70
   5. Solving Nonlinear Optimization Problems 71
   6. Conclusions 84

Contributors 87

Chapter 1

Testing the Efficiency of Foreign Exchange Market – Part 1

Chris Czerkawski* and Osamu Kurihara**
*Faculty of Economic Sciences, Hiroshima Shudo University
1-1 Ozuka-Higashi 1-chome, Asaminami-ku, Hiroshima, Japan 731-3195
** Graduate School of Engineering, Hiroshima University
1-4-1 Kagamiyama, Higashi-Hiroshima City Hiroshima, Japan 739-8527

Abstract

Testing the Efficient Market Hypothesis (EMH) usually includes a joint hypothesis. The first one, the rationality hypothesis assumes that the realized future spot rate is the sum of the expected spot rate and the random error term. Then, the asset pricing assumes that the forward rate is the sum of the anticipated spot rate and a time-varying risk premium. Consequently most empirical research focused on the speculative efficiency hypothesis when the risk premium is assumed zero. It also assumed that that forward prices are the best unbiased forecast of future spot prices is often presented in the economic and financial analysis of futures markets. If a market is subject to efficient speculation, the supply of speculative funds is infinitely elastic at the forward price that is equal to the expected future spot price. The expected future spot price is a market price determined as the solution to the underlying rational expectations macroeconomic model.

In this research we use methodology developed by Corbae (1987) which is based on the cointegration model and allows the existence of stationarity and risk-free premium to test a condition for efficiency in selected time periods in the forward market[1]. Part one of this paper will provide an introduction to the topic and part two development of the applied theory and methodology. In second stage, not included in this paper, we will discuss empirical aspects of testing for non-stationarity and tests for a sine qua non condition for market efficiency.

Key Words: Efficient Market Hypothesis (EMH), Speculative Efficiency Hypothesis, Expected Future Spot Price

1. Introduction and Review of Literature

The existing tests of the efficiency in the forward market usually included three basic forms of the EMH. The weak-form EMH implies that the market is efficient, reflecting all market information. This hypothesis assumes that the rates of return on the market should be independent; past rates of return have no effect on future rates. With this assumption, usual conditions such as the traders use to buy or sell a stock, are invalid. The semi-strong form EMH implies that the market is efficient, reflecting all publicly available information. This hypothesis assumes that stocks adjust quickly to absorb new information. The semi-strong form EMH also incorporates the weak-form hypothesis. Given the assumption that stock prices reflect all new available information and investors purchase stocks after this information is released, an investor cannot benefit over and above the market by trading on new information. The strong-form EMH implies that the market is efficient: it reflects all information both public and private, incorporating the weak-form EMH and the semi-strong form EMH. Given the assumption that stock prices reflect all information (public as well as private) no investor would be able to profit above the average investor even if he was given new information.

The existing tests on forward market efficiency are numerous. For example, the Vector Autoregression (VAR) approach is claimed by Hallwood and MacDonald (1994) to be more efficient than single equation regression in the study of spot and forward rate relationships[2]. Here the advantages of a VAR model are debated in non-standard way. First, it does not treat the forward rate as being exogenous as single equation models do. Dynamic relatioship between changes in the spot rate and in the forward rate may be allowed, which is empirically possible. Second, lagged changes in both spot and forward rates are explicitly incorporated to provide a complete analysis. Serially correlated residuals in single equation models may totally or partly reflect those lagged variables, but it is not clear what this serial correlation is about—serial correlation in single equations is a matter to be corrected to obtain right estimates of parameters, rather than useful elements in an information set.

An alternative way of testing Foreign Exchange Market Efficiency Hypothesis is based on the Behavioral Equilibrium Exchange Rate (Clark & MacDonald, 1998). The FOREX market will be efficient if fully reflects all available information. If this holds, the actual exchange rate will not deviate significantly from its equilibrium rate. The proposed methodology concentrates on the statistical properties of the misalignment rate.

Another approach differs from the single equation approach in the way it handles the issues raised above. It treats the forward exchange rate as being endogenous, in a (dynamic) system, which is close to reality and to agents' behaviour. It proves that there is a role for lagged changes in exchange rates, which bring more changeable components to the right hand side of the equations. Unlike other studies including news components, either multiplicative or additive, on the right hand side of the regression equation to increase the variability in a random fashion, our approach suggests that the variability is systematically built in, and regulated by exchange rate dynamics[3].

Goss (1985) tested the joint hypothesis of spot and futures prices on the LME from 1966 to 1984. He rejected the EMH for copper and zinc, but not for lead and tin. Sephton and Cochrane (1990) investigated the EMH for the LME with respect to six major base metals using monthly overlapping data from 1976 to 1989[4]. They found that the LME is an inefficient market. Sephton and Cochrane (1991) reconsidered the LME data over the same period using the CUSUM of Squares stability test[5]. They showed that the LME experienced structural change over this period, which implied that the market efficiency tests based on the Fama research scheme were somewhat less than conclusive (Sephton and Cochrane 1990). Data from 1976–1987. They found that the EMH could not be rejected for copper and lead, but could be rejected for tin and zinc. In line with the cointegration method, Kenourgios and Samitas (2004) explored Int. J. Financial Stud. 2018, 6, 32 3 of 10 the 3-month and 15-month maturities of copper futures contracts from 1989 to 2000 found that the copper futures market was not efficient[6]. Using the cointegration approach, Arouri et al. (2011) studied aluminum on the LME and investigated both short- and long-run efficiency, and they showed that the futures aluminum price was cointegrated with the spot price, which was then a biased estimator of the future spot price.

Otto (2011) analyzed the EMH of the LME using 3M (the most liquid futures contract on the LME) and 15-month (15M) futures prices from July 1991 to March 2008 with the monthly average second ring price data. He rejected the null hypothesis of speculative efficiency for all base metals with the exception of aluminum. He argued that one reason for aluminum's efficiency may have been due to aluminum being the most liquid on the LME. For the 15M contracts, he failed to reject the null hypothesis for the six major base metals except for lead and tin. He noted that a possible reason for rejecting the hypothesis for lead and tin is in their illiquidity. Due mainly to trading reality, brokers usually calculate the futures prices based on the most liquid 3M futures contract prices (Otto 2011). Using the 15M futures prices to analyze the EMH seems to be irrelevant. As the concept of market efficiency seems to require somewhat sufficient liquidity, the 15-month tenor data analysis cannot satisfy the principles of arbitrage. Thus, this paper focused on 3M futures rather than 15M futures[7].

The efficiency of futures markets is critical to their price informative function. Some papers test for both long-run and short-run efficiency using cointegration and error correction models. Variance-bounds tests are developed and utilized for examining the question of efficiency. Results often show that the market is efficient and provides an unbiased estimate of future spot prices for one and two months away from expiration. However, for three and more months away from expiration this is not the case, which has implications for the users of this market. Chinn and Coibion (2014) investigated the unbiasedness of futures prices in major commodity markets such as energy, precious metals, base metals, and agricultural commodities using the statistical relationship between the basis and ex-post price changes. In particular, they considered the major base metals aluminum, copper, lead, nickel, and tin (not zinc) through Bloomberg. The monthly data they used in their study started in July 1997. They found that the futures prices of precious and base metals implied a strong rejection of the null hypothesis of unbiasedness, while the futures prices in the energy and agricultural markets were consistent with unbiasedness[8].

In summary, there is no consensus regarding the efficiency of the LME. Empirical evidence to date is mixed; for any given market, some studies find evidence of efficiency, others of inefficiency. In part, these apparently conflicting findings reflect differences in the time periods analyzed and the methods chosen for testing. A limitation of existing tests is the classification of markets as either efficient or inefficient with no assessment of the degree to which efficiency is present.

Some studies have been criticized for using incorrect econometric methodology (Otto 2011). Furthermore, most studies have utilized monthly data, which cannot appropriately capture the arbitrage possibilities in the futures markets. In particular, there has been some discussion regarding how average data may lead to spurious results (Gross 1988)[9]. This paper therefore applied the previously used Canarella and Pollard (1986) methodology to most updated recent and high-frequency data, or daily data, to reflect the market arbitrage possibilities that institutional investors face[10]. However, there is evidence that the long-run relationship does not hold in the short run; specifically, changes in the spot price are explained by lagged differences in spot and futures prices as well as by the basis. This suggests that market inefficiencies exist in the sense that past information can be used by agents to predict spot price movements.

In this paper the methodology originally developed by Corbae and others (1987) will be used to test the sine qua non condition for efficiency of the market with regard to several Asia-Pacific markets that include a model of pricing with stationary risk premium. At the later stage data on forward and spot markets will be sampled weekly to obtain more detail in the parameter estimates. Also much larger sample of maturities for the selected foreign exchange forward market will be analyzed.

The rest of the paper will present the theoretical side of the problem and the applied methodology.

2. Methodology

The tests of the EMH are often conducted based on the following model with the first part of hypothesis

(1) $S_t - a + bF_{t-1} + et$

Where S_t is the spot price in the time t, F_{t-1} is the price at time t-1 for the forward or futures contract maturing at time t ; et is an error term with the mean zero and the finite variance, and a and b are constant coefficients. Here bF_{t-1}, t may be regarded as the expectation factor at time t. Lower case letters involving exchange rates denote that they are in natural logarithms. Also a 0 and b 1 which assumes that the hypothesis is unbiased. Originally developed by Hansen and Hodrick (1980) and known as the simple efficiency hypothesis as the test for unbiased hypothesis is a test market efficiency and no-risk premium.

The second part of the hypothesis is usually defined as following

(2) $t_{t,n} = E_t(S_{t+n}) + RP_t$

Where $t_{t,n}$ is the ne-period forward rate at time t and RP_t is the risk premium at time t. S_{t+n} is the logarithm of the spot rate. The second equation also suggests that agents are risk averse and require risk premium before entering any forward purchase. Fluctuations of the agent's revenue stream occur because the principal's equipment unit can be either in state 0 ('operational') or in state 1 ('down'). In the operational state the penalty rate is 0, whereas in the lower condition the penalty rate is p. In other words, the penalty rate at any point of time can be modelled as pB where B is a Bernoulli random variable. The Bernoulli distribution is a discrete distribution having two possible outcomes labelled by $n=0$ and $n=1$ in which $n=1$ ("success") occurs with probability p and $n=0$ ("failure") occurs with probability $q=1-p$, where $0<p<1$. It therefore has probability density function of value 0 with probability $P(0)=\mu/(\lambda+\mu)$ and value 1 with probability $P(1)=\lambda/(\lambda+\mu)$. The dispersion of B decreases as $P(1)$ moves away from 1/2 in either direction. Denote momentarily $a \equiv P(1)$. Under the null hypothesis, none of the variables included in the Z_{t-j} set help to explain S_{t+1}.

In other words, the efficient expectations hypothesis holds well. Cornell (1977) and Bilson (1981) were the first to make use of a direct test of the hypothesis and considered that the forward rate is an observable series of expectations. Frankel (1980) considered a model of the form[11]:

(3) $S_{t+1} = \alpha + \beta f_t + \mu_{t+1}$

The hypothesis of efficiency is accepted if $\alpha = 0$ and $\beta = 1$ hold simultaneously. Many researchers have estimated and assessed the efficiency hypothesis (e.g. Bilson, 1981; Baillie et al., 1983; Bailey et al., 1984; Hsieh, 1984; Baillie, 1989; McCurdy and Morgan, 1991). The method of testing the above model was either ordinary least squares (OLS) or instrumental variable estimations (IVE) (Frenkel, 1981) with lagged forward rates, a time trend and interest rate differentials as the employed instruments. Instrumental variables estimates are generally inconsistent if the instruments are correlated with the error term in the equation of interest. As Bound, Jaeger, and Baker (1995) note, another problem is caused by the selection of "weak" instruments, instruments that are poor predictors of the endogenous question predictor in the first-stage equation. In this case, the prediction of the question predictor by the instrument will be poor and the predicted values will have very little variation. Consequently, they are unlikely to have much success in predicting the ultimate outcome when they are used to replace the question predictor in the second-stage equation. The majority of the results have clearly shown that the forward rate is not an unbiased predictor of the corresponding future spot rate[12].

The problem of efficiency may be examined in terms of the 'news' model proposed by Frenkel (1980, 1981) and modified by Apergis and Eleftheriou (1997)[13].

To test the efficiency hypothesis with a 'news' model the following equation is regressed:

(4) $s_{t+j} - s_t = \alpha + \beta(E_t s_{t+j} - s_t) + \gamma news_{t+j} + \mu_{t+j}$

Where $E_t s_{t+j}$ represents the expected spot rate at period t+j given any available information at period t, and news represents the difference between a function of some fundamentals at time t+j and their expected value at time t. In most studies $E_t s_{t+j}$ is replaced by the forward rate f_t. According to Eq. [4], changes in the spot exchange rate occur because of new information which has not been anticipated in the previous period.

News is a function of j–1 innovations that occur in the prediction interval from period t+t+1. In other words, $E(news_{t+j} news_{t+j+k}) = 0$ for k >1. With regard to the significance of coefficient γ in Equation [4], a statistically insignificant γ indicates that exchange rate fluctuations do not react to new information, thus indicating that this new information has already been incorporated to exchange rate movements, i.e. the exchange rate market is efficient.

Additionally, Frenkel (1981) generated news as the residuals from another regression as a proxy for news and to use them as a separate regressor in (4) and we discussed the limit of this approach. Therefore a proxy for 'news' can be used from residuals in a vector autoregressive (VAR) model, the same conducted by Baillie (1987).

A VAR model in a standard form can be written as follow:

(5) $X_t = A_0 + A_1 X_t + \mu_t$

or a multivariate generalization of [5]:

(6) $X_t = A_0 + A_1 X_{t-1} + A_2 X_{t-2} + \cdots A_p X_{t-p} + \mu_t$

where
X_t= is an (n×1) vector containing each of n variables included in the VAR
A_0= is an (n×1) vector of intercept terms
A_1= is an (n×n) matrices of coefficients
μ_t= is an (n×1) vector of error terms

A VAR model is usually a better technique than any structural equation model, since macroeconometric models are not usually based on sound economic theories and the VAR model, may be employed, which do not impose rigid a priori restrictions on the data generation process (Lutkepohl, 1993). In other words, the user of a VAR model imposes few restrictions and usually employs OLS estimation. A VAR model is also largely free of the uncertain specification assumptions and errors associated with traditional macro econometric procedures, so it can capture certain dynamic relationships among any economic variables better than the standard macro econometric models.

Nevertheless, considerable controversy has dealt with certain limitations of the VAR approach (Cooley and Leroy, 1985; Leamer, 1985)[14].

This controversy has mainly focused on the specific accidental ordering of the variables involved in the VAR model. It is generally believed that, for results to be considered conclusive, they must be strictly systematic to ordering in order to identify unexpected shocks. In order to obtain a relationship between interest rate differential 'news' and exchange rate surprises, it is also useful to decompose the general model into a more specific one. Estimating a level VAR model including non-stationary variables is estimating the impulse response functions to capture the dynamic responses of non-policy variables due to unexpected shocks in the policy variables. The unexpected shocks can be identified by decomposition' that imposes a recursive structure on the model or alternatively the policy shocks can be identified by imposing 'theory driven restrictions' on the contemporaneous relationships among the variables concerned[15].

Notes

[1] Corbae, D. S Oularis and J. F Zander, Testing a Necessary Condition for Efficiency in the Foreign Exchange Market, Working Paper No. 88-24, Department of Economics, University of Maryland, 1987.

[2] Hallwood, C.P., MacDonald, R., 1994. International Money and Finance, 2nd ed. Blackwell, Oxford, Cambridge, MA. Testing for efficiency and rationality in foreign exchange markets—a review of the literature and research on foreign exchange market efficiency and rationality with comments Peijie Wang, Trefor Jones, Journal of International Money and Finance No.21 (2002) p. 223–239.

The proposed methodology concentrates on the statistical properties of the misalignment rate. Considering a Logistic Smooth Transition Autoregressive (LSTAR) model we test whether a nonlinear STAR model or a linear autoregressive model should be estimated. This test is applied to three Central & Eastern European Countries – members of the EU. In each case, we examine exchange rates per EURO to find whether these rates imply efficient foreign exchange markets. This research used VAR method as its approach, which has impulse response and variance decomposition to obtain the variables dynamics. Results from Augmented Dickey-Fuller and Phillips-Perron unit root test confirmed that all variables are stationer in level; hence, the VAR method that being employed is VAR in level. Clark, P.B. and R. MacDonald, (1999), "Exchange Rates and Economic Fundamentals: A Methodological Comparison of BEERs and FEERs" in R. MacDonald and J Stein (eds) Equilibrium Exchange Rates, Kluwer: Amsterdam. And IMF Working Paper 98/67 (Washington: International Monetary Fund, March 1998).

[3] Hallwood, C., MacDonald, R., (1994). International Money and Finance. Blackwells, Oxford. Chapters 11 & 12.Vector autoregression (VAR) is a stochastic process model used to capture the linear interdependencies among multiple time series. VAR models generalize the univariate autoregressive model (AR model) by allowing for more than one evolving variable. All variables in a VAR enter the model in the same way: each variable has an equation explaining its evolution based on its own lagged values, the lagged values of the

other model variables, and an error term. VAR modeling does not require as much knowledge about the forces influencing a variable as do structural models with simultaneous equations: The only prior knowledge required is a list of variables which can be hypothesized to affect each other intertemporally. The VAR approach to modelling foreign exchange rate behaviour is proposed by Hakkio (1981)Hakkio, 1981 and Baillie et al. (1983). Baillie (1989), Baillie and McMahon (1989), MacDonald and Taylor (1990a,b) are among this category. The hypothesis of efficiency implies a set of cross-equation restrictions imposed on the parameters of the time series model. This paper derives these restrictions, proposes a maximum likelihood method of estimating the constrained likelihood function, estimates the model and tests the validity of the restrictions with a likelihood ration statistic. See Craig Hakkio, Expectations and the Forward Exchange Rate, NBER Working Paper No. 439, 1980.

[4] Goss, Barry A., ed. 1985. The Forward Pricing Function of the London Metal Exchange. In Futures Markets: Their Establishment and Performance. London: Routledge, pp. 157–173. The proposed methodology concentrates on the statistical properties of the misalignment rate. Considering a Logistic Smooth Transition Autoregressive (LSTAR) model test were performed whether to check if nonlinear STAR model or a linear autoregressive model should be estimated. This test was applied to three Central & Eastern European Countries – members of the EU. In each case, we examine exchange rates per EURO to find whether these rates imply efficient foreign exchange markets. This research used VAR method as its approach, which has response and variance decomposition to obtain the variables dynamics. Results from Augmented Dickey-Fuller and Phillips-Perron unit root test confirmed that all variables are stationary in level; hence, the VAR method that being employed was VAR. See, Clark, P.B. and R. MacDonald, (1999), "Exchange Rates and Economic Fundamentals: A Methodological Comparison of BEERs and FEERs" in R. MacDonald and J Stein (eds) Equilibrium Exchange Rates, Kluwer: Amsterdam. And IMF Working Paper 98/67 (Washington: International Monetary Fund,March 1998).

[5] Sephton, Peter S., and Donald K. Cochrane. 1991. The Efficiency of the London Metal Exchange: Another Look at the Evidence. *Applied Economics* 23: 669–674.

[6] Kenourgios, Dimitris, and Aristeidis Samitas. 2004. Testing Efficiency of the Copper Futures Market: New Evidence from London Metal Exchange. Global Business and Economics Review, Anthology. pp. 261–271. Available online:
https://papers.ssrn.com/sol3/papers. 27 February 2018).

[7] Otto, Sascha Werner. 2011. A Speculative Efficiency Analysis of the London Metal Exchange in a Multi-Contract Framework. *International Journal of Economics and Finance* 3: 3–16.

[8] Chinn, Menzie D., and Olivier Coibion. 2014. The Predictive Content of Commodity Futures. *The Journal of Futures Markets* 34: 607–636.

[9] Gross, Martin. 1988. A Semi-Strong Test of the Efficiency of the Aluminum and Copper Markets at the LME. *The Journal of Futures Markets* 8: 67–77.

[10] Canarella, Giorgio, and Stephen K. Pollard. 1986. The "Efficiency" of the London Metal Exchange: A Test with Overlapping and Non-Overlapping Data. *Journal of Banking and Finance* 10: p. 575–593. Hansen, L.P. and Hodrick, R.J. (1980) Forward Exchange Rates as Optimal Predictors of Future Spot Rates: An Econometric Analysis. *Journal of Political Economy*, 88, 829-853. The authors found that the financial market integration would increase international nonsynchronous trading effects (INTE), in general, and the impact monotonically decreases over the lag length. However empirical evidence suggests that the increase is asymmetric among developed and emerging markets. Further theoretical investigation revealed that the level of volatility and autocorrelation are positively related to the increase in INTE. The paper concludes that the

relatively higher level of volatility and autocorrelation in emerging markets could mitigate the increase in INTE from financial market integration.

[11] Instrumental variable methods allow for consistent estimation when the explanatory variables (covariates) are correlated with the error terms in a regression model. Such correlation may occur 1) when changes in the dependent variable change the value of at least one of the covariates ("reverse" causation), 2) when there are omitted variables that affect both the dependent and independent variables, or 3) when the covariates are subject to non-random measurement error. Explanatory variables which suffer from one or more of these issues in the context of a regression are sometimes referred to as endogenous. In this situation, ordinary least squares produces biased and inconsistent estimates. Cornell B, Spot Rates, forward rates and exchange market Efficiency, Journal of Financial Economics, No. 5, p. 55-65; Bilson J.F.O, The Speculative Efficiency Hypothesis, Journal of Business, No 54, p. 435-451; Frenkel I.A., Exchange Rates, Prices and Money, *American Economic Review*, No 70, p. 235-242

[12] Bound, John, David A. Jaeger, and Regina M. Baker, 1995, "Problems with Instrumental Variables Estimation When the Correlation Between the Instruments and the Endogenous Explanatory Variable is Weak," *Journal of the American Statistical Association*, 90(430): 443-50 See also Gregory, A. W. and Mc Curdy T. H. The unbiasedness hypothesis in the forward foreign exchange market: A specification analysis with application to France, Italy, Japan, the United Kingdom and West Germany, *European Economic Review*, Vol 30, No 2, April 1986, p. 365-381 Brenner and Kroner [Brenner, R., Kroner, K., 1995. Arbitrage, cointegration, and testing the unbiasedness hypothesis in financial markets. *Journal of Financial and Quantitative Analysis* 30, pp. 23–42] argue that the cointegration condition is rarely met in practice. They attribute this outcome to potentially non-stationary net cost-of-carry which would make the parameters of the cointegration relation unstable. It is for this reason that Hansen's tests of the stability of the parameters in cointegration regressions were used to supplement more traditional cointegration tests. Baillie, Richard T.; Bollerslev, Tim. "Common Stochastic Trends in a System of Exchange Rates," *Journal of Finance*, 44, March 1989, pp. 167–181.

[13] The news model was tested using quarterly data on six exchange rates involving four currencies over a period extending back to 1975. The results show that unbiased efficiency does not hold and that there are time-varying risk premia. The results also show that the news variables, proxied by the residuals of VAR models, do not have a significant effect on the exchange rate. It is argued that while news is a theoretically plausible explanation for erratic changes in the exchange rate, generated regressors cannot adequately represent news. Frankel, Jeffrey A. "Tests of Rational Expectations in the Forward Exchange Market," *Southern Economic Journal*, 46, April 1980, pp. 1083-101, Apergis, N. and S. Eleptheriou (2001) 'Measuring price elasticity of aggregate demand in Greece: 1961-1995', *Public Finance Review*. See also Apergis, N. and Eleftheriou, S. (2001) 'Stock returns and volatility: evidence from the Athens Stock Exchange Market Index', *Journal of Economics and Finance* 25, 50-61.

[14] This paper shows that the exclusion restrictions used to identify structural vector autoregressions (SVARs) generally give inconsistent parameter estimates under rational expectations. These strong restrictions may explain why rational-expectations models are frequently rejected by the data. Cooley and LeRoy, 1985. Thomas A. Cooley, Stephen F. LeRoy. A theoretical macroeconomics: A critique. *Journal of Monetary Economics*, 16 (1985), pp. 283-308. Gordon and King, 1982.. E. Leamer, Sensitivity Analyses Would Help. American Economic Review 1985, vol. 75, issue 3, 308-313, ibidem. Also H. Lutkepohl, Introduction to multiple time series analysis. Springer Verlag. Berlin and New York, 1991. p.194-197. The common criticism of the VAR approach includes two points; First, assuming that plausible losses will be less than some multiple (often three) of VAR - losses can be extremely large. And second, reporting a VAR that has not passed a

backtest. Backtesting is the process of testing a trading strategy on relevant historical data to ensure its viability before the trader risks any actual capital. A trader can simulate the trading of a strategy over an appropriate period of time and analyze the results for the levels of profitability and risk. Regardless of how VAR is computed, it should have produced the correct number of breaks (within sampling error) in the past. A common violation of common sense is to estimate a VAR based on the unverified assumption that everything follows a multivariate normal distribution.

[15] A system of equations is recursive rather than simultaneous if there is unidirectional dependency among the endogenous variables such that, for given values of exogenous variables, values for the endogenous variables can be determined sequentially rather than jointly. Due to the ease with which they can often be estimated and the temptation to interpret them in terms of causal chains, recursive systems were the earliest equation systems to be used in empirical work in the social sciences. A recursive model is a special case of an equation system where the endogenous variables are determined one at a time in sequence. Thus the right-hand side of the equation for the first endogenous variable includes no endogenous variables, only exogenous variables. The right-hand side of the equation for the second endogenous variable includes exogenous variables and only the first endogenous variable. The right-hand side of the equation for the third endogenous variable includes exogenous variables and only the first and second endogenous variables, and so on. Another way to put this is to say that a system is recursive if the solution for the *g* th endogenous variable involves only the first *g* equations. See International Encyclopedia of Social Sciences, available on line https://www.encyclopedia.com/social-sciences/applied-and-social-sciences-magazines/recursive-models

Chapter 2

Global Flow of Funds and Uncertainty: Focus on the Cross-Border Financing[1]

Nan Zhang* and Li Zhu**
*Faculty of Economic Sciences, Hiroshima Shudo University
1-1 Ozuka-Higashi 1-chome, Asaminami-Ku, Hiroshima, 731-3195 Japan
**Southwestern University of Finance and Economics.
555 Liutai Road, Wenjiang District, Chengdu, 611130, P.R.China

Abstract

This paper tries to clarify global uncertainty from the view of the global flow of funds by investigating the uncertain shocking influence of Cross-Border Financing between China, Japan, and the U.S. using the Bank for International Settlements (BIS) Locational Banking Statistics data. The dyadic structure of this data allows to disentangle supply and demand factors and to better identify the effect of uncertainty shocks on cross-border banking flows. The results of this analysis suggests that: (i) uncertainty is both a push and pull factor that robustly predicts a decrease in both outflows (retrenchment) and inflows (stops); (ii) global banks rebalance their lending towards safer foreign borrowers from local borrowers when facing higher uncertainty; (iii) this rebalancing occurs only towards advanced economies (flight to quality), but not emerging market economies.

Keywords: Global Flow of Funds, Cross-Border Financing, Statistical Matrix, Portfolio Rebalancing, Financial Stability

1. Introduction

Global Flow of Funds (GFF) is the external flow of funds that relate to domestic and

---

[1] This research was supported by the grants-in-aid for scientific research (Scientific Research C, 16KT0185).

international capital flows. GFF concept is an extension of the domestic flow of funds. It connects domestic economies with the rest of the world. GFF data could provide valuable information for analyzing interconnectedness across borders and global financial interdependencies. In order to promote the research on GFF statistics, we submitted the discussion paper (Zhang, 2015) to the 2015 IARIW-OECD Conference. This paper primarily discusses three issues of GFF statistics: the relationship between GFF and the SNA statistical system, its statistical framework, and its data sources and methods. To continue this research, we organized a Special Topic Session for the 60th ISI WSC (STS027) in 2015. At the session, Zhang's paper (2016) discussed the definition of GFF, the theoretical framework of GFF statistics, and its integration in the preparation of data sources. However, due to the lack of rigorous integration of the original data, that paper lacks a systematic relationship to the accounts in this paper. In addition, we also organized an invited session for the Society for Economic Measurement's 2017 Conference. The main purpose of this session was to measure GFF and apply it to regular monitoring of GFF. We had discussed related problems, such as GFF's data sources, its statistical framework, and the analysis method. Through the author's research work as a visiting scholar in the statistics department at Stanford University since 2014, we have completed the design of the GFF statistical framework, integrated its data sources, and tentatively compiled the statistical matrix (stock) table of the end of 2015 and the end of 2016 (Zhang, 2018).

The growing incidence of financial crises and their damage to economies has led policymakers to sharpen their focus on financial stability analysis. Recently, the IMF had a working paper[2] that noted that statisticians are responding to the growing interest in this topic by calling for measuring GFF. The Data Gaps Initiative (DGI) has not made a specific recommendation to develop a GFF; the work is still in an embryonic stage.

In view of the existing works that have been carried out in this domain and the gaps therein, we aim to present a new statistical approach to measure GFF, including an empirical example to illustrate its operational potential. To measure financial stress and observe triggers and spillovers of systematic financial crises through GFF, it is necessary to strengthen the research on GFF statistical methods.

In order to measure global uncertainty and financial stress and observe the spillover effects of systematic financial crises through GFF, in this paper, we focus on the application of GFF statistics. Using GFF statistics, we can observe interlinkages of counterparties and transmission channels of cross-border capital flows to analysis the vulnerabilities from financial positions, risk build-up, and causes and effects of imbalances. This can provide a basis for decision making for financial policy authorities.

The remainder of the paper is organized as follows. Section 2 briefly describes the statistical framework of GFF and the prepared GFF matrix table. Section 3 describes the data on cross-border financing which taken out from the GFF matrix, together with data on uncertainty

---

[2] Robert Heath and Evrim Bese Goksu, "Financial Stability Analysis: What are the Data Needs?" IMF Working Paper WP/17/153, (2017), 54.

Table 1. Global Flow of Funds Matrix for a Country

		a	b	c	d	e	f	g	
Holder of liability (creditor) / Issuer of liability (debtor)	Financial Instruments	Country A	Country B	Country C	...	All Other Economies	Total Liabilities of Financial Instruments	Total Liabities	
Country A	Direct investment								1
	Portfolio investment								2
	Financial derivatives								3
	Other investment								4
Country B	Direct investment								5
	Portfolio investment								6
	Financial derivatives								7
	Other investment								8
Country C	Direct investment								9
	Portfolio investment								10
	Financial derivatives								11
	Other investment								12
......	......								13
All other economies	Direct investment								14
	Portfolio investment								15
	Financial derivatives								16
	Other investment								17
Total Asset of Financial Instruments	Direct investment								18
	Portfolio investment								19
	Financial derivatives								20
	Other investment								21
Total Asset									22
Net Worth									23
Reserve assets									24
Monetary gold									25
Special drawing rights									26
Reserve position in the fund									27
Other reserve assets									28
Adjustment item									29
Net Financial Position									30

Notes: (i) Net worth is the difference between assets and liabilities (2008SNA, P29).

(ii) Adjustment item is an item for balancing the net worth, reserve assets and net financial position in GFFM, and put it in row 29. It is derived from the net worth of each county by:

a. Adjustment item = Net Financial Position - Net Worth - Reserve assets, and

b. Net Financial Position = Net Worth + Reserve assets + Adjustment item

and various macroeconomic controls. Section 4 proposes the econometric methodology used in this paper to mitigate endogeneity issues and disentangle between credit demand and supply factors, and presents the main results and a battery of robustness exercises. Section 5 concludes.

2. Statistical Framework and Global Flow of Funds Matrix

Table 1 is in accordance with IIP statistical standards and is based on a structure wherein the from-whom-to-whom data are used to establish the GFF statistical framework and is in keeping with the double-entry principle. According to the statistical standards of IIP, which are based on BPM6, the IIP can be set as foreign financial assets and external debt. Each column corresponds to the balance sheet of a country in question, with country, assets, and liabilities then listed in rows by an instrument with the counterparty country identified for each cell.

Table 1 provides a statistical framework for deriving the GFF matrix. Assets are subdivided into five parts: direct investment, portfolio investment, financial derivatives, other investments, and reserve assets. Liabilities are divided into four parts: direct investment, portfolio investment, financial derivatives, and other investments. The net financial position is external financial assets plus reserve assets minus liabilities. By this statistical framework, the GFF statistics can reflect stock information of financial assets and liabilities between the world and a region at a particular time. Importantly, the GFF statistics remain consistent with IIP Statistics Standard, while also exhibiting unique methodological characteristics, which can be summarized as follows:

(1) In order to reflect the relationship between from-Whom-to-Whom (W-to-W), GFF statistics use the parallel processing method wherein transaction and countries (sectors) are rows, namely, by putting the Table 1. Global Flow of Funds Matrix for a Country transaction item that direct investments, securities investments, financial derivatives, and other investments to countries (sectors) in the rows, whereas each country (sector), is in the columns. Accordingly, we can determine the dual relationship of a transaction item in countries (sectors), which can show the scale of the position item and reflect from-whom-to-whom-by-what relationships in a two-way format. For example, a5–a8 in the table shows Country A transactions in the columns by showing which financial instruments are used for transactions bringing how much funds to country B. As this can provide two-way information about the financing structure of Country A with country B, we also can identify and understand the financing scale and corresponding information on counter parties. At the same time, we can also capture information of where country A is located in the row vectors from other countries to raise funds. We can also acquire relevant information on country B in the row vectors on its fund-raising from Country A, Country C, etc.

(2) To reflect the actual situation of international capital in a country or a region, and in order to establish the GFF matrix table for the application analysis, we set countries (sectors) in rows and columns by the principle of W-to-W tabulating. We also designed an "all other economies" sector (see column e and row 9–12 that can be represented as e9, e10, e11, e12).

The relationship of these "all other economies" and the world total can be expressed as follows: "liabilities of all other economies" = total liabilities − liabilities of the total for specific countries. That is, $e9 = f9 - (a9 + b9 + c9 + d9)$, ... , $e12 = f12 - (a12 + b12 + c12 + d12)$.

(3) Each "column" shows a country how to use funds by transaction item, namely, who outputs how much funds by what item; each "row" represent how a country raises funds through four financial instruments, namely, who inputs how much funds by what item. The difference between the total of the row and column in row 23, which shows the balance between the use of external funds financing for a certain country at a particular point in time, that is, the net output of funds. For instance, Country A's net worth equals country A's total assets minus its total liabilities, that is, $a23 = a22 - (g1 + g2 + g3 + g4)$.

(4) Corresponding to the various transaction instruments of various countries rows 24–28 show part of the reserve assets, specifically monetary gold, special drawing rights, reserve positions in the fund, and other reserve assets. Denoting reserve assets as an instrument in Table 3 shows a balanced relationship between net worth and net financial position and the components thereof. For example, country A's component of reserve assets can be shown as $a24 = a25 + a26 + a27 + a28$.

(5) The bottom row in Table 3, namely rows 30, reflects net IIP, corresponding to Table 3's Net Financial Position that obtained each country. These data are taken from IIP and reflect overall equilibrium conditions of national external financial positions. Theoretically, adding reserve assets to the net worth of the financial assets of a country should reveal the external net financial position of the country. For example, $a30 = a23 + a24$, and $b30 = b23 + b24$..., etc. However, since there are factors, like the non-compatibility of IIP data and other datasets and the difficulty in selecting the financial-investment item, the actual external net financial investment figures are inconsistent with the above theoretical relationship. Therefore, in order to attain balance when adding the net worth in row 23 to the reserve assets in row 24 so they are equal to the financial position in row 30 of Table 3, we need to set up an adjustment item for balancing the net worth, the reserve assets and net financial position in GFFM, and put is in row 29. Net financial position of each country is calculated using net worth, i.e., net financial investment plus reserve assets and adjustment item is equal to net financial position, such as $a30 = a23 + a24 + a29$, $b30 = b23 + b24 + b29$, ..., $e30 = e23 + e24 + e29$.

(6) Because the main purpose of compiling the GFF matrix table is to observe cross-border capital positions, the diagonal line elements in the matrix are zero. Each position is the result of financial investment between the domestic and foreign countries, and does not include a country's internal financial investments.

(7) In the thick line box at the top half of Table 3, if the financial instruments of each country in rows are merged, we can get a square matrix, with the same number of rows as columns, and an orthogonal matrix can be obtained. So we can use this orthogonal matrix to make some statistical inferences about actual cases.

The statistical framework delineated in Table 1, and the corresponding data sources, can provide information about fund-raising. It can indicate financial stability, comparability across

GFF within a country and across countries, and the spread effect for taking corresponding financial policies on domestic and global financial markets. On the basis of this, Table 1 can also break down further some special needs of financial supervision, based on the W-to-W, to compile a separate matrix for measuring each financial instruments, such as the Table 2.

In addition, using the form of W-to-W to comply with the GFF matrix can also improve the quality and consistency of data, providing more opportunities for cross-checking and balancing information. When linking information with Table 1 and Table 2, we can map the bilateral relationship between a country and a regional economy at a specific point in time. The GFF matrix, which is built using stocks data, can also be extended to flow data, to quantify bilateral flows of funds, but it also then needs to determine the following three factors: (1) volume of transactions; (2) valuation of financial assets and liabilities; and (3) other changes in volume of assets and liabilities. Using Table 1 and Table 2, we can find that the previous statistical information cannot clear the synthesis problems, namely "what is the main section on bilateral financing, what financial instruments are used, and what is the structure and scale of bilateral financing?" Based on the statistical framework, we will discuss the data sources and then give a case of bilateral countries to illustrate the method of compiling the GFF matrix model.

Table 2. Financial Instrument Matrix on a W-to-W Basis

Counterpart Countries (Investment from)	Counterpart Countries (Investment in)				
	Country A	Country B	...	All other Economies	Total of the World
Country A					
Country B					
...					
All other Economies					
Total of the World					

Based on the layout of Table 1, this section discusses how to create external stock matrices. As an example, Table 3 shows what may be possible in a GFF framework for a country to enable monitoring of financial positions at both region/nation and cross-border levels through financial instruments. Table 3 also based on W-to-W benchmark, the "column" as an Assets, and "row" represents liabilities. The matrix here has the same number of rows as columns too, which a square matrix.

Table 3 is an illustration of the GFF matrix as of the end of December 2016. Each row of the matrix has two statistical groupings, including countries and three financial instruments for showing the source of funds, that is, direct investment (DI), portfolio investment (PI) and other investment (OI), covering the main structural elements of external financial liabilities. Financial assets are listed by country in the columns to show fund uses, with the counterparty sectors identified for each cell. The columns of the matrix delineate 14 sectors, that is, 11 country

Table 3. External Asset and Liabilities Matrix for the End of 2016 (millions of USD)

Issuer of liability (debtor)	Financial Instruments	Canada	China	France	Germany	Italy	Japan	Korea	Netherlands	Switzerland	United Kingdom	United States	Other	Total of Financial Instruments	Total Liabilities
Canada	Direct investment		15933	6002	11591	1005	21673	1088	69608	41110	31128	292002	123464	614604	
	Portfolio investment		5553	25813	48142	4041	70860	4881	23673	36807	55454	826639	387153	1489016	2688771
	Other investment		7969	18912	22917	1010	44280	1226	7337	5860	70300	188528	216811	585150	
China	Direct investment	10001		22191	60404	7054	142021	95068	29221	11439	19390	70120	2067623	2534532	
	Portfolio investment	13749		13470	3510	436	15445	11522	12020	4484	40919	107805	606704	830064	4120600
	Other investment	6041		32168	19124	1067	52114	38749	7122	2680	52331	29419	515189	756004	
France	Direct investment	4021	1935		63817	19737	16154	839	92986	73634	81927	57187	285343	697579	
	Portfolio investment	33303	5431		359306	150859	252108	12083	179248	76318	202251	482972	1159813	2913691	5671994
	Other investment	5097	14473		193096	67031	190958	1725	92396	56137	397420	88815	953576	2060724	
Germany	Direct investment	2398	2313	45526		35418	22968	5114	146029	64989	66523	74792	319980	786051	
	Portfolio investment	35534	6558	212441		79907	123469	6158	215459	83842	200214	372832	1405912	2742327	5536561
	Other investment	8047	18395	112586		68574	92105	3167	78201	53942	406278	44706	1122183	2008184	
Italy	Direct investment	96	-10	62647	29520		2899	404	67952	17685	45350	8748	109458	344749	
	Portfolio investment	6542	1079	253093	159755		53148	1244	39178	8835	63398	92112	472337	1150721	1936659
	Other investment	0	624	169825	73854		28964	495	15356	7105	71516	4378	69072	441189	
Japan	Direct investment	1328	885	27984	3383	1013		3419	22230	10457	12985	52215	54645	190544	
	Portfolio investment	60270	11894	98948	23920	5450		14737	52485	26596	263692	861587	621939	2041518	5686792
	Other investment	16466	30479	185334	18409	493		6562	3791	5843	297463	447235	2442655	3454730	
Korea	Direct investment	2202	5576	4205	6951	325	43505		17581	3419	14086	31778	45723	175350	
	Portfolio investment	14747	2700	8394	7836	549	23934		11696	9198	36215	179534	194346	489150	876563
	Other investment	518	21559	9388	3484	24	31729		0	2116	16913	15857	110476	212064	
Netherlands	Direct investment	31081	23827	125078	217940	102944	79262	2348		279504	357744	758146	2105959	4083833	
	Portfolio investment	19565	3100	258758	238844	54492	116360	4174		68477	151937	448078	595437	1959223	7089089
	Other investment	5291	0	97339	158942	11566	64424	837		24382	240554	54265	388433	1046033	
Switzerland	Direct investment	-172	0	37212	24762	4762	5168	0	317138		50729	122028	424097	985724	
	Portfolio investment	24062	4345	24519	48592	8455	28263	4552	21008		82263	430555	219215	895827	2665162
	Other investment	684	2337	57199	62477	4201	22985	990	20701		214665	59821	337551	783611	
United Kingdom	Direct investment	19276	2673	81821	81712	4098	56170	2342	162198	53878		452475	471630	1388273	
	Portfolio investment	77039	14457	232128	189062	65760	166578	20586	107874	74092		1182407	1192991	3322974	9119092
	Other investment	54000	67640	332931	320428	86907	254770	5669	288385	169534		684582	2142998	4407844	
United States	Direct investment	371468	27475	252864	291697	30010	421103	40937	355242	310759	555687		1068176	3725418	
	Portfolio investment	793370	125687	255673	364398	105045	1595299	139742	473853	293416	1075336		6983607	12205426	20598669
	Other investment	310732	100803	249946	153439	38690	1195123	30524	117308	90892	974775		1405593	4667825	
Other	Direct investment	335788	496503	399250	462269	136368	415005	54987	1956115	485663	1123941	2134424		14807862	
	Portfolio investment	218762	178856	1130488	1533421	810782	1432246	83081	606807	578461	1396565	4777138		19376996	40840073
	Other investment	82695	409688	876305	581373	157075	533244	143397	288849	456783	1629881	1669501		6655215	
Total Asset of Financial Instruments	Direct investment	777486	577109	1064781	1254046	342733	1225928	206546	3236300	1352538	2359490	4053914	13883648	30334519	106830026
	Portfolio investment	1296944	359659	2513726	2976787	1285776	3877710	302761	1743301	1260525	3568244	9761659	20469841	49416934	
	Other investment	489571	673967	2141933	1607543	436638	2510696	233341	919446	875274	4372096	3287107	9530961	27078573	
Total Asset		2564001	1610735	5720439	5838375	2065147	7614334	742648	5899047	3488337	10299830	17102680	43884451	106830026	
Net Worth		-124769	-2509865	48445	301814	128488	1927543	-133915	-1190043	823175	1180738	-3495989	3044378		
Reserve assets		82718	3097845	146770	185287	136043	1220418	371103	36166	679620	134642	407223			
Monetary gold		0	67878	90645	125705	91241	28592	4795	22824	38780	11505	301090			
Special drawing rights		7578	9661	10166	15755	6894	18087	2887	6031	4335	10261	48882			
Reserve position in the fund		2191	9597	5157	6941	2634	11959	1719	1433	1319	6699	18385			
Other reserve assets		72949	3010708	40802	36886	35275	1161781	361701	5878	635186	106177	38865			
Adjustment item		170400	1212557	-565207	1314216	-438526	-159030	41298	1654918	-732272	-1422134	-5239612			
Net Financial Position		128349	1800537	-369991	1801316	-173995	2988881	278485	501042	770523	-106753	-8318378			

Data Source: IMF, Coordinated Direct Investment Survey (CDIS), Coordinated Portfolio Investment CPIS), http://www.imf.org/external/data.htm, and International Investment Position Statistics (BOP/IIP) http://data.imf.org/?sk=7A51304B-6426-40C0-83DD-CA473CA1FD52&sId=1409773422141, BIS international banking statistics, http://stats.bis.org/statx/toc/LBS.html on 2/20/2018.

sectors, all other economies, the total of financial instruments, and total liabilities. The total of all sector's assets or liabilities is equal to the total assets or liabilities of the world. The columns of the matrix are configured to understand the external assets for many countries, thereby displaying both national and regional perspectives. Each column corresponds to the balance sheet of the sector in question; which countries or regions should appear in the matrix depends on the specific purpose of the analysis. The data in Table 3 are derived from IMF Data Warehouse and BIS' IBS. But FD data are not used in Table 3 because many countries lack such data.

Table 3 can further indicate the scope of external financing conditions, such as (1) the proportion of and relationship with the international financial market; (2) the risk of imbalance in external financial assets and liabilities; an (3) transmission route of impacts from the outbreak of a financial crisis in a country or region as well as a country to enable implementation of an effective financial policy in terms of the impacts arising from other countries. For brevity, we focus on China, Japan, and the United States to trace the effects of external financing such as cross-border banking flows.

According to the framework of Table 2, in order to meet the special tracking analysis of a financial investment, first, we created a matrix for measuring a financial instrument, namely the matrix of cross-border banking investment, as shown in Table 4.

The BIS compiles and publishes two sets of statistics on international banking activity, namely the Locational Banking Statistics (LBS) and Consolidated Banking Statistics (CBS). This paper use data on cross-border claims and liabilities from LBS as our main source, because these statistics provide information about the currency composition of banks' balance sheets and the geographical breakdown of their counterparties. The LBS data capture outstanding claims and liabilities of internationally active banks located in reporting countries against counterparties residing in more than 200 countries. Banks record their positions on an unconsolidated basis, including intragroup positions between offices of the same banking group. The data is compiled following the residency principle that is consistent with the balance of payments (BOP) statistics, and compatible with IIP, CDIS, and CPIS. In this regard, the major advantage of the BIS' LBS data, compared to the banking flows collected from the balance of payments statistics, is the detailed breakdown of the reported series by counterparty countries. This feature enables us to identify changes in the supply factors of banking flows from changes in demand for bank credit in counterparty countries.

Table 4 uses the data of LBS that published by the BIS, which includes 12 countries and regions and "Other Economies" that have a larger proportion of the global banking credit market and greater influence on international politics and economies. Table 4 includes "Other Economies" defined as described above. It is a matrix table based on a W-to-W benchmark: the columns show assets, and the rows represent liabilities. The matrix is a square matrix, with the same number of rows as columns, which is an orthogonal matrix. We can use the matrix to make various statistical estimates for meeting the needs.

Table 4. Cross-Border Financing Matrix (millions of USD, as of end-2016)

Claims \ Liabilities	Canada	China	France	Germany	Italy	Japan	Korea	Netherlands	Switzerland	United Kingdom	United States	Other Economies	Total of World	Net Assets	Total L.
Canada		7969	18912	22917	1010	44280	1226	7337	5860	70300	188528	216811	585150	0	585150
China	6041		32168	19124	1067	52114	38749	7122	2680	52331	29419	515189	756004	0	756004
France	5097	14473		193096	67031	190958	1725	92396	56137	397420	88815	953576	2060724	81209	2141933
Germany	8047	18395	112586		68574	92105	3167	78201	53942	406278	44706	1122183	2008184	0	2008184
Italy	0	624	169825	73854		28964	495	15356	7105	71516	4378	69072	441189	0	441189
Japan	16466	30479	185334	18409	493		6562	3791	5843	297463	447235	2442655	3454730	0	3454730
Korea	518	21559	9388	3484	24	31729		0	2116	16913	15857	110476	212064	21277	233341
Netherlands	5291	0	97339	158942	11566	64424	837		24382	240554	54265	388433	1046033	0	1046033
Switzerland	684	2337	57199	62477	4201	22985	990	20701		214665	59821	337551	783611	91663	875274
United Kingdom	54000	67640	332931	320428	86907	254770	5669	288385	169534		684582	2142998	4407844	0	4407844
United States	310732	100803	249946	153439	38690	1195123	30524	117308	90892	974775		1405593	4667825	0	4667825
Other Economies	82695	409688	876305	581373	44536	533244	143397	288849	456783	1629881	1669501		6655215	2875746	9530961
Total of World	489571	673967	2141933	1607543	436638	2510696	233341	919446	875274	4372096	3287107	9530961			
Net Liabilities	95579	82037	0	400641	4551	944034	0	126587	0	35748	1380718	0			
Total A.	585150	756004	2141933	2008184	441189	3454730	233341	1046033	875274	4407844	4667825	9530961			

Data Source: BIS, https://www.bis.org/statistics/about_banking_stats.htm, June 20, 2018.

Table 4 has the following four characteristics. First, by using the form W-to-W, we can observe and analyze the bilateral relations of relevant countries in cross-border banking credit; the elements on the diagonal are zero, which means that the matrix does not include domestic banking credit. Second, we can understand the structure of the global banking credit market, and the proportion and influence of relevant countries in the securities market. Third, using the banking assets located in a column and subtracting the liabilities in each row, we can see the net assets and the relevant information of the counterparty. Fourth, Table 4 shows the balance position on assets and liabilities for each country and the global market in banking credit. The specific instructions for using Table 4 are as follows: if the net assets figure is positive, a zero appears in the net row, which indicates the net liabilities of the corresponding country. If the net assets figure is negative, a zero appears in the net column, which indicates the net assets of the corresponding country. After this processing, we can see the balance, that is, the total of each row is equal to the total of each column, and the sum of the rows in the matrix equals the sum of the columns.

Among international financial trading instruments, compared with direct investments, securities investment and financial derivative, the liquidity of cross-border banking credit are the fastest. Because a large number of private banking are also operating in the banking market, the possibility of a financial crisis is the highest when the credit chain is interrupted due to the occurrence of a default. Therefore, it is important to observe the demand and supply of a country's external credit funds to control cross-border banking credit and stabilize the international financial market and prevent a financial crisis. In the next section, we will use the matrix data to do an empirical analysis.

3. Data Sources for Measuring Cross-Border Financing

The BIS compiles and publishes two sets of statistics on international banking activity, namely the Locational Banking Statistics (LBS) and Consolidated Banking Statistics (CBS). This paper uses data on cross-border claims and liabilities from LBS[3][3] as our main source, because these statistics provide information about the currency composition of banks' balance sheets and the geographical breakdown of their counterparties. The LBS data capture outstanding claims and liabilities of internationally active banks located in reporting countries against counterparties residing in more than 200 countries. Banks record their positions on an unconsolidated basis, including intragroup positions between offices of the same banking group. The data is compiled following the residency principle that is consistent with the balance of payments (BOP) statistics, and compatible with International Investment Position (IIP), Coordinated Direct Investment Survey (CDIS) and Coordinated Portfolio Investment Survey (CPIS). In this regard, the major advantage of the BIS' LBS data, compared to the banking flows collected from the balance of payments statistics, is the detailed breakdown of the reported series by counterparty countries. This feature enables us to identify changes in the supply factors of banking flows from changes in demand for bank credit in counterparty countries.

Currently, banking offices located in 47 countries, including many offshore financial centers, report the LBS. The LBS capture around 93 percent of all cross-border interbank business (Bank for International Settlements, 2017)[4]. The BIS' LBS provides the exchange-rate adjusted flows in cross-border bank claims and liabilities, while the Consolidated Banking Statistics (CBS) based on the nationality principle does not have information on currency breakdown. The adjustment for exchange rate movements is particularly important because contractions in cross-border banking flows tend to coincide with large currency movements and heightened uncertainty. Thus, ignoring the valuation effect could bias the results of the effect of uncertainty shocks on cross-border banking flows.

Cross-border financing refers to any financing arrangement that crosses national borders. Cross border financing could include cross border loans, letters of credit or bankers acceptances (BA), for example, issued in the United States for the benefit of a person in Japan. This paper

---

[3] The BIS locational banking statistics (LBS) are reported by banking offices located in selected countries, including many offshore financial centers, and exclude the assets and liabilities of banking offices outside of these countries. The number of LBS-reporting countries increased from 14 in 1977 to 47 in 2017.

[4] Although there is no similar estimate for the share of cross-border bank lending to non-banks in the LBS, Adjiev et al. (2017) claim that it is likely to be above 90 percent.

will analyze the cyclical pattern of gross capital flows, focusing on the effect of uncertainty shocks on cross-border banking flows. According to the theory of economics, we can know that the LBS data structure allows us to control for time-variant unobserved factors in recipient countries, we need to control for macroeconomic variables in source countries to identify the causal effect of uncertainty shocks on the cross-border banking flows, so the following variables are selected as explanatory variables for measuring cross-border banking credit: Cross-Border Claims (CBC), Cross-Border Liabilities (CBL), the Inflation Rate (CPI), Domestic Credit to Private Sector (% of GDP, RDCP), External Debt to GDP ratio (EDG), Nominal Effective Exchange Rate growth (NEER), Real GDP Growth Rate (RGGR), Stock Market Growth (SMG), the Monetary Policy Rate (R)[5]

4. Econometric Model and Empirical Findings

4.1 Statistical description

First, we need to make a statistical descriptive observation of the cross-border banking credit between China, Japan, and the United States to master their basic characteristics. Table 5 is compiled from Table 4, which can show the relationship on cross-border banking credit between China, Japan, and the United States. Similarly, the rows of the matrix represent liabilities, and the columns represent claims.

Table 5 focuses on cross-border banking credit between China, Japan, and the United States, there are the following three main points. First, it can show the credit balance on cross-border banking position, we can know that the credit balance by from-whom-to whom. At the end of 2016, China lent $52.2 billion from Japan, $29.4 billion from the United States and

Table 5. Cross-Border Financing Matrix of China, Japan, and the United States

	China	Japan	The U.S.	Other	Total of World	Net Assets	Total Liabilities
China		52114	29419	674471	756004	0	756004
Japan	30479		447235	2977016	3454730	0	3454730
The U.S.	100803	1195123		3371899	4667825	0	4667825
Other	542685	1263459	2810453	13583417	18200014	2406789	20606803
Total of World	673967	2510696	3287107	20606803			
Net Liabilities	82037	944034	1380718	0			
Total Assets	756004	3454730	4667825	20606803			

Data Source: BIS, LBS. Table A6.2-S, June 20, 2018; Note: The data unit is millions of USD, end-2016.

---

[5] NEER is used by Trade Partners by Consumer Price Index. R is used by Interest rates, discount, and percent per annum. NEER which is Trade Partners by Consumer Price Index, and an increase in the nominal exchange rate denotes the depreciation of local currencies against the U.S. dollar. SMG's distinction is as below: for China, Shanghai stock exchange composite index; for Japan, Tokyo Nikkei 225 index; for the United States, Dow Jones Industrial Average.

$674.5 billion from other economies through international bank credit. And at the same time, China also loaned $30.5 billion to Japan, $100.8 billion to the United States and $542.7 billion to other economies. In the same way, we can also know the cross-border banking credit positions between Japan and the United States. Japan lent $447.2 billion from the United States and $2977 billion from other economies. And at the same time, Japan also loaned $1195 billion to the United States, $1263 billion to other economies. The second point is that the United States accounts for the largest proportion in international banking credit, and the scale of international banking credit between Japan and the United States is much larger than of China and Japan or China and the United States. The third point is that at the end of 2016, China, Japan, and the United States were both net external liabilities in cross-border banking credit, and the United States cross-border banking net borrowing reached $1380 billion.

Table 5 reflects the situation of cross-border banking credit at the end of 2016 with the stock data, in order to give the long-term changes in cross-border banking credit between China, Japan, and the United States, we have drawn Figure1 with using the time series data from 1995 to 2017. The left axis in Figure1 represents a stock market index, and the right axis in Fig.1 shows cross-border bank capital outflows and inflows.

Figure1 shows fluctuations in the stock market index with total cross-border claims and liabilities for China, Japan, and the U.S. Three observations stand out from this figure. First, the different scales of the y-axis in these graphs demonstrate the dominance of the U.S. and Japan in the global banking system. Compared to the U.S. or Japan, the size of cross-border banking flows into/from China that is one of the largest emerging market economies is not as strong as the real economy suggests. Second, the figure shows that heightened uncertainty in a local economy is often associated with a reduction in both cross-border bank claims and liabilities. Third, the slowdown and growth in cross-border banking flows during the Global Financial Crisis (GFC) is at the unprecedented level in all three countries, consistent with the findings from the recent literature (Ahmed and Zlate, 2014; Cerutti et al., 2015b; Passari and Rey, 2015; Correa et al., 2017; Sangyup and Davide, 2018).

Identifying the effect of uncertainty shocks on cross-border banking flows is challenging because it is hard to separate between credit demand and credit supply factors. For example, to properly quantify the effect of uncertainty shocks on cross-border lending one would have to control for all possible macroeconomic shocks affecting credit demand in recipient countries. We overcome this challenge by using data on bilateral cross-border bank claims and liabilities from the BIS' LBS database.

Figure 2 shows the mutual credit relationship in cross-border banking flows between China, Japan, and the United States. In Figure 2, a), namely "the U.S.-China", shows the credit changes of cross-border Banks between the United States and China. "Cross-border claims" means the claims of the United States to China's bank credit, and "Cross-border liabilities" means the liabilities of the United States to China's bank credit. In other words, the liabilities of the United States to China is also the claims of China to the United States in this case.

To illustrate the dyadic structure, Figure 2 presents examples of bilateral cross-border

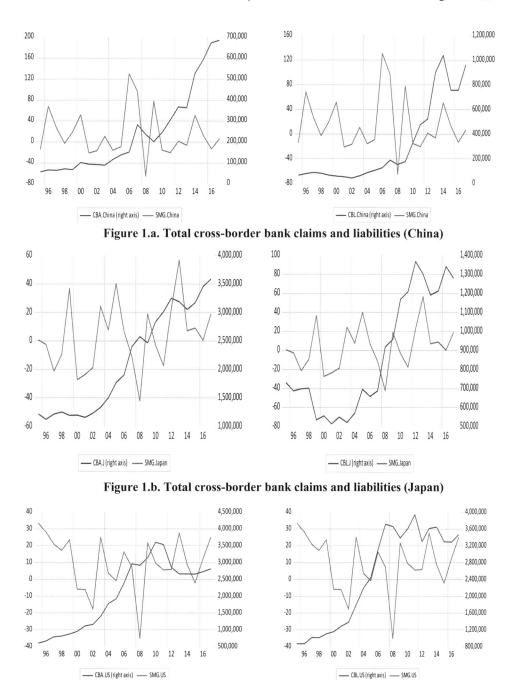

Figure 1.a. Total cross-border bank claims and liabilities (China)

Figure 1.b. Total cross-border bank claims and liabilities (Japan)

Figure 1.c. Total cross-border bank claims and liabilities (The U.S.)

Notes: CBA is cross-border assets, CBL is cross-border liabilities (millions of USD); SMG is stock market growth. We use Shanghai stock exchange composite index for showing the market volatility in China, Tokyo Nikkei 225 index for Japan, and Dow Jones Industrial Average for the United States.

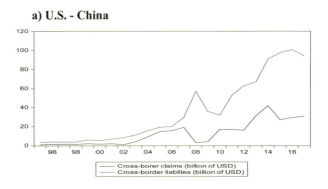

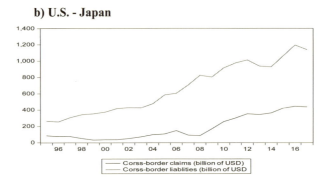

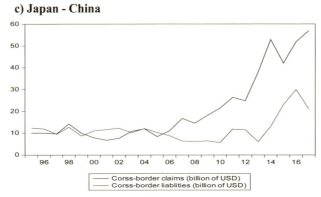

Fig. 2. The bilateral cross-border bank claims and liabilities

Data Source: BIS, LBS. Table A3

claims and liabilities between the three countries (the U.S., Japan, and China). Compared to Figure 1, Figure 2 presents some heterogeneity in the pattern of cross-border claims and liabilities among different in the U.S., Japan, and China. At the individual country-pair, the correlation between cross-border claims and liabilities is high, and the U.S. is a net borrower for both Japanese and Chinese banking credit, Japan has high assets in cross-border banking credit and steady growth, and China still accounts for a low proportion of the international banking credit market. Another feature is that the large increase in cross-border banking credit between China, Japan, and the United States after the global financial crisis in 2007, and the cyclical pattern of the flows differs between advanced and emerging market economies.

4.2 Econometric Model

As a country's external claims and liabilities, we can regard it as the external fund demand and supply. Any empirical study of the factors affecting bank credit must note that changes in the volume of credit reflect not only supply-side factors but also demand-side factors. Because demand for credit is also responsive to changes in macroeconomic conditions, including uncertainty, which, in turn, affects the expected returns and risks on investment projects. We use the dyadic structure of LBS data (that is, multiple reporting countries linked to multiple counterparties) to control the unobserved time-variant factors in a counterparty country, thereby effectively control all possible demand-side factors. This method clearly identifies the role of uncertainty as both a push factor and pull factor in cross-border banking credits.

To speculate the impact of higher uncertainty in a local economy on determining cross-border claims (i.e., a push factor), we first estimate the following equation:

$$\Delta CBC_{i,j,t} = \alpha_{j,t} + \beta_1 CPI_{i,t} + \beta_2 NEER_{i,t} + \beta_3 R_{i,t} + \beta_4 RDCP_{i,t} + \beta_5 RGGR_{i,t} + \beta_6 SMG_{i,t} + \varepsilon_{i,j,t} \quad (1)^6$$

where i and j respectively indicate the reporting ('source') and counterparty ('recipient') countries, and t denotes time. This paper's main dependent variable $\Delta CBC_{i,j,t}$ denotes the quarterly growth (log difference) in cross-border claims of banks in a country I in a country j; $\alpha_{j,t}$ are recipient country-time fixed effects, included to control for any macroeconomic shocks affecting recipient countries, including external and idiosyncratic recipient-specific shocks as well as indirect impact of uncertainty through other recipient countries. In addition, the inclusion of counterparty-time fixed effects effectively maximizes the sample size of our analysis because many of counterparty countries do not necessarily have data on every control variable. And β is the coefficient of our interest. A negative (positive) β indicates that global banks decrease (increase) cross-border lending in an absolute term when the local economy faces higher uncertainty.

One main advantage of the BIS LBS data is that the currency composition of cross-border claims and liabilities is available so that cross-border banking flows expressed in U.S. dollars are adjusted for movements in exchange rates. To the extent that heightened uncertainty episodes coincide with large fluctuations in the exchange rate, it is crucial to obtain a real measure of cross-border flows. Because the BIS LBS reports the stock data, we used the quarterly stock data of the cross-border claims ($L_{i,j,t}$), and take the log difference to obtain the

---

[6] CBC: Cross-Border Claims; CPI: Inflation, average consumer prices, percent change; NEER: Nominal Effective Exchange Rate, Trade Partners by Consumer Price Index; R: Financial, Interest Rates, Discount, Percent per quarter; RDCP: Domestic credit to private sector (% of GDP); RGGR: Real GDP growth rate; SMG: Stock Market Growth (the detailed definition of SMG is the same as the notes in figure 1)

growth rate $\Delta CBC_{i,j,t}$

Follow the same logic, we also analyze the effect of higher uncertainty in a source country on cross-border liabilities of its banking sector, by replacing the stock of the cross-border claims ($\Delta CBC_{i,j,t}$) in equation (1) with the stock of the cross-border liabilities ($CBL_{i,j,t}$):

$$\Delta CBL_{i,j,t} = \alpha_{j,t} + \beta_1 CPI_{i,t} + \beta_2 NEER_{i,t} + \beta_3 R_{i,t} + \beta_4 RDCP_{i,t} + \beta_5 RGGR_{i,t} + \beta_6 SMG_{i,t} + \varepsilon_{i,j,t} \quad (2)$$

Again, we focus on China, Japan, and the U.S. only due to the asymmetry in the LBS data. In this case, a negative (positive) β indicates that global banks receive less (more) cross-border lending in an absolute term when their home country faces higher uncertainty.

4.3 Statistical Inference and Analysis

Table 6 shows the results obtained by estimating equation (1) and (2). We discuss the results of estimating equation (1) first, and then we present the results of estimating equation (2). Due to the limited availability of some control variables, we start presenting a specification which includes only the inflation rate (CPI), Nominal Effective Exchange Rate growth (NEER), Monetary Policy Rate (R), Domestic credit to private sector (% of GDP, RDCP), real GDP growth rate(RGGR), stock market growth (SMG) as controls.

The signs of control variables are largely consistent with the previous findings regarding the determinants of international capital flows. For example, once controlling for credit demand, global banks in a country with higher economic growth lend more to foreign borrowers. It is because the health of the banking system improves with the domestic economic condition, enabling them to expand lending activity. Domestic monetary policy tightening has a positive effect on gross cross-border claims. Although the conventional bank lending channel of monetary policy implies that tighter monetary policy in a local economy induces banks to reduce their lending, the economic expansion in the local economy accompanied by monetary policy increases cross-border lending. The depreciation of local currencies with respect to the U.S. dollar is associated with a slowdown in cross-border bank lending. Nevertheless, the effect is not robust in our sample.

Table 6 shows some characteristics of cross-border bank credit between China, Japan, and the U.S. Importantly, higher uncertainty in a home country reduces gross cross-border bank claims (retrenchment), and this effect is both economically and statistically significant. For example, an increase in the level of uncertainty from the historical median to the level observed during the global financial crisis is associated with an increase in cross-border claims of 6.74-17.69 percentage points. In column China, we can know that CPI, NEER, and RDCP have a positive effect on the cross-border claims, but the monetary policy rate has a negative effect. The influence of GDP growth rate and stock market growth is not statistically significant. In column Japan and the U.S., we can see that domestic credit to the private sector of GDP have a significant impact on cross-border claims, but Japan has a negative impact, which the U.S. has a positive impact. Similarly, the GDP growth rate of Japan and the U.S. is not statistically

Table 6. Statistical inference for the impact on cross-border banking credit

	Growth of Cross-border Claims			Growth of Cross-border Liabilities		
	China	Japan	The U.S.	China	Japan	The U.S.
C	6.7401	17.6931	10.4739	6.7359	17.6882	10.4660
	(5.005)	(46.719)	(14.321)	(5.003)	(46.958)	(14.383)
CPI inflation	0.1217	0.1069	0.0894	0.1215	0.1076	0.0897
	(3.999)	(2.026)	(0.892)	(3.993)	(2.085)	(0.900)
Nominal Effective Exchange Rate growth (NEER)	0.0578	0.0108	0.0025	0.0577	0.0107	0.0027
	(3.811)	(1.915)	(0.155)	(3.809)	(1.915)	(0.1701)
Monetary Policy Rate (R)	-0.1518	0.6515	-0.1024	-0.1516	0.6473	-0.1022
	(-2.433)	(2.282)	(-2.546)	(-2.430)	(2.279)	(-2.554)
Domestic credit to private sector (% of GDP, RDCP)	0.0418	-0.0194	0.0227	0.0418	-0.0194	0.0228
	(6.818)	(-8.624)	(6.784)	(6.820)	(-8.653)	(6.831)
Real GDP Growth Rata (RGGR)	0.0535	-0.0069	-0.0283	0.0539	-0.0070	-0.0289
	(0.864)	(-0.279)	(-0.669)	(0.870)	(-0.285)	(-0.686)
Stock Market Growth (SMG)	0.0019	0.0041	0.0037	0.0019	0.0041	0.0037
	(1.0434)	(2.179)	(0.853)	(1.025)	(2.178)	(0.865)
Obs	23	23	23	23	23	23
R-squared	0.9127	0.8497	0.8757	0.9127	0.8507	0.8769

Note: The model used annual data from 1995 to 2017. The dependent variables are the growth rate of cross-border claims in column China, Japan to the U.S. and the growth rate of cross-border liabilities in column China, Japan to the U.S. All independent variables are lagged by one period. T-statistic are put in parentheses. Standard errors are clustered at the reporting-counterparty country levels with denotes 5% significance level.

significant. Despite the reduced sample size due to the limited availability of these variables, the effect of domestic uncertainty shocks on cross-border bank lending remains broadly unchanged.

On the other hand, in column China, Japan and the U.S. in the growth of cross-border liabilities, we summarize the same set of results for cross-border liabilities of a reporting country. In other words, we examine whether higher uncertainty in a local country reduces gross inflows to the domestic banking sector (stops). In column China, higher CPI inflation, Nominal effective exchange rate growth and domestic credit to the private sector of GDP in the reporting countries are associated with an increase in cross-border bank liabilities, but monetary policy rate will reduce the inflows of cross-border, although higher real GDP growth and stock market growth is no longer statistically significant. Importantly, the sign of uncertainty is negative and statistically significant, suggesting that uncertainty reduces gross inflows to the domestic banking sector.

Compared with China, Japan's CPI, monetary rate, and stock market have promoted the inflows of bank financing, which is statistically significant, but RDCP shows a negative correlation. When we look at the U.S. column, we can know that the U.S. policy rate will reduce the bank capital inflows is the same as that of China, the higher RDCP helps the capital inflows of foreign banks.

Especially, through the speculation results of the monetary policy rate, we can know that the size of coefficients found in China tends to be larger than that in Japan and the U.S., implying that the negative effects of uncertainty shocks on the cross-border banking flow into China are larger than those into Japan and the U.S. This finding is consistent with a large body of empirical literature that capital flows into emerging market economies are more procyclical than advanced economies (Raddatz and Schmukler, 2012).

5. Conclusion

Based on the GFF framework, this paper develops an empirical analysis of cross-border bank credit by using the systematic approach of statistical description and reasoning. The main findings are as follows.

First, this paper establishes and prepares the statistical framework of GFF. Based on this framework, we integrated the sample data of 12 countries and regions and compiled the external financial assets and liabilities matrix the end of 2016. Secondly, the cross-border bank credit is separated from the comprehensive external financial assets and liabilities matrix, and the cross-border bank financing matrix is established. Third, the focus of the analysis is focused on the cross-border credit in China, Japan, and the U.S. to construct a cross-border financing matrix based on W-t-W benchmark, and the statistical description and analysis are carried out on the basis of this matrix. Fourth, using LBS and related data to establish the cross-border bank financing model, from the claims and the liabilities two sides carried out on the statistical analysis of China, Japan, and the U.S. external financing characteristic, found that the Chinese foreign bank financing cycle is longer than Japan and the U. S., and its instability is also higher than in Japan and the U.S.

Because the LBS data structure allows us to control for time-variant unobserved factors in recipient countries, we need to control for macroeconomic variables in source countries to identify the causal effect of uncertainty shocks on the cross-border banking flows. Based on the extensive literature on international capital flows, we consider the following set of controls: real GDP growth, stock market growth, the inflation rate, the monetary policy rate, nominal exchange rate growth, private credit growth, and the external debt to GDP ratio. This paper is just an attempt to focus on cross-border bank financing analysis based on the GFF analysis framework. Although an observational cross-border bank financing model is established according to the characteristics of LBS data, given the large cross-section data and short time series, the predicted results are not very satisfactory. Developing a new analysis method for panel data analysis is a subject to be studied in the future.

References

[1] Ahmed, Shaghil, and Andrei Zlate. "Capital flows to emerging market economies: A brave new world?" *Journal of International Money and Finance* 48 (2014): 221-248.

[2] Avdjiev, Stefan, Bryan Hardy, Sebnem Kalemli-Ozcan, and Luis Servén. "Gross capital inflows to banks, corporates, and sovereigns," No. w23116. National Bureau of Economic Research (2017).

[3] Bank for International Settlements, http://www.bis.org/statistics/consstats.htm. Sep. 5, 2017. Cerutti, Eugenio, Galina Hale, and Camelia Minoiu. "Financial crises and the composition of cross-border lending." *Journal of International Money and Finance* 52 (2015b): 60-81.

[4] Correa, Ricardo, Teodora Paligorova, Horacio Sapriza, and Andrei Zlate. "Cross-Border Bank Flows and Monetary Policy," Working Paper of Federal Reserve Board (2017).

[5] Established Principal Global Indicators (PGI) Website:
   http://www.principalglobalindicators.org/default.aspx, Sep. 10, 2016.

[6] Financial Stability Board and International Monetary Fund "The Financial Crisis and Information Gaps," Report to the G-20 Finance Ministers and Central Bank Governors (2009).

[7] Gourio, Francois, Michael Siemer, and Adrien Verdelhan. "Uncertainty and international capital flow," Working paper (2016).
   https://site.stanford.edu/sites/default/files/capital_flows_april24_2016.pdf

[8] IMF, Balance of payments and international investment position manual, 6th Edition (BPM6) (2014).

[9] 一, http://www.imf.org/external/data.htm

[10] 一, http://data.imf.org/?sk=40313609-F037-48C1-84B1-E1F1CE54D6D5&ss=1393552803658

[11] 一, http://data.imf.org/?sk=B981B4E3-4E58-467E-9B90-9DE0C3367363

[12] 一, Update of the Monetary and Financial Statistics Manual (MFSM) and the Monetary

and Financial Statistics Compilation Guide (MFSCG) (2016).

[13] —, Balance of Payments and International Investment Position Compilation Guide (2017).

[14] IMF, BIS and ECB, Handbook on securities statistics (2015).
http://www.imf.org/external/np/sta/wgsd/pdf/hss.pdf. March 10, 2017.

[15] Luca Errico, Richard Walton, Alicia Hierro, Hanan AbuShanab, Goran Amidzic, "Global Flow of Funds: Mapping Bilateral Geographic Flows," Proceedings 59th ISI World Statistics Congress, 2825-2830 (2013).

[16] Luca Errico, Artak Harutyunyan, Elena Loukoianova, Richard Walton, Yevgeniya Korniyenko, Goran Amidžić, Hanan AbuShanab, Hyun Song Shin, "Mapping the Shadow Banking System Through a Global Flow of Funds Analysis," IMF Working Paper, WP/14/10, (2014).

[17] Manik Shrestha, Reimund Mink, and Segismundo Fassler, "An Integrated Framework for Financial Positions and Flows on a From-Whom-to-Whom Basis: Concepts, Status, and Prospects," IMF Working Paper WP/12/57 (2012).

[18] Nan Zhang, "New Frameworks for Measuring Global-Flow-of-Funds: Financial Stability in China," in the 32nd General Conference of The International Association for Research in Income and Wealth (IARIW) (2012).

[19] —, Measuring Global Flow of Funds and Integrating Real and Financial Accounts, Working paper, 2015 IARIW-OECD Conference: W(h)either the SNA? April 16-17, 2015.
http://www.iariw.org/c2015oecd.php

[20] Raddatz, Claudio, and Sergio L. Schmukler. "On the international transmission of shocks: Micro-evidence from mutual fund portfolios," *Journal of International Economics* 88.2 357-374 (2012).

[21] Robert Heath and Evrim Bese Goksu, Financial Stability Analysis: What are the Data Needs? IMF Working Paper, WP/17/153 (2017).

[22] Sangyup Choi and Davide Furceri, "Uncertainty and Cross-Border Banking Flow," IMF Working Paper WP/18/4 (2018).

[23] Shrestha, Manik, Reimund Mink and Segismundo Fassler, "An Integrated Framework for Financial Positions and Flows on a From-Whom-to-Whom Basis: Concepts, Status, and Prospects," IMF Working Paper WP/12/57 (2012).

[24] WEF (World Economic Forum), & Vital Wave Consulting, Big Data, Big Impact: New Possibilities for International Development. World Economic Forum. Retrieved August 24, 2012.http://www.weforum.org/reports/big-data-big-impact-new-possibilities-international-development

[25] Zhang, N., The Global Flow of Funds Analysis in Theory and Application, Minerva-Shobo, pp. 31-67 (2005).

[26] —, "New Frameworks for Measuring Global-Flow-of-Funds: Financial Stability in China," the 32nd General Conference of The International Association for Research in Income and Wealth (IARIW). http://www.iariw.org/c2012.php, Aug. 20, 2012.

[27] —, "Measuring Global Flow of Funds: Theoretical Framework, Data Sources and Approaches" Kyushu University Press, pp. 47-60 (2016).

[28] —, "Measuring Global Flow of Funds: Statistical Framework, Data Sources, and a Country Case," Discussion paper, 4th Annual Conference of The Society for Economic Measurement, MIT, July 26-8, 2017. https://sem.society.cmu.edu/MIT.html

[29] —, Big Data techniques for Measuring Global Flow of Funds, *Recent Studies in Economic Sciences,* Kyushu University Press, 47-60 (2018).

[30] —, "Measuring Global Flow of Funds: A Case Study on the U.S., Japan, and China," the 35th General Conference of The International Association for Research in Income and Wealth (IARIW). http://www.iariw.org/c2018copenhagen.php, (2018).

Chapter 3

Assessing the Fiscal Impact of Trade Liberalization in Laos: A General Equilibrium Approach

Sithanonxay Suvannaphakdy[+] and Toshihisa Toyoda[*]
[+]*Laos-Australia Development Learning Facility,*
Level 2, Vieng Vang Tower, Boulichan Road, PO Box 468, Vientiane Capital, Lao PDR
[*] *Center for Social Systems Innovation, Kobe University*
and Professor Emeritus, Hiroshima Shudo University

Abstract

Trade liberalization entails the transition from trade taxes to domestic taxes. Certain structural characteristics such as narrow tax base and significant proportion of subsistence sectors, however, constrain such transition and hence reducing public revenues in developing countries. This paper contributes to this debate by assessing the impact of trade liberalisation on domestic tax revenue in Laos. We find that Laos has been able to recover revenue loss from tariff reduction through the introduction of value-added tax (VAT). VAT generated LAK 5,510 billion or 30% of tax revenue in 2017, which was about twice higher than the ratio of tariff revenue to tax revenue in 2000. Our simulation results of tariff liberalization using a computable general equilibrium (CGE) model also reveals that further reduction in tariff rate will be associated with lower indirect tax rate. In particular, the 20% tariff reduction will increase private consumption by 1.14%, but will decrease the effective indirect tax rate from 6.2% to 5.2% and reduce tax revenue by 11%. The worsening tax revenue loss reflects the non-optimal indirect tax rate, which needs to be reduced by 11%. The key policy implication is that any policy designed for raising tax revenue should aim at improving tax collection system and broadening tax base rather raising indirect tax rate.

Key Words: Trade liberalization, Fiscal impacts, Domestic tax revenue, Laos, CGE model

1. Introduction

How much should domestic tax revenue change in response to tariff liberalization? For policy makers, this question became a focus of study after the seminal works by Mitra [16] and Greenaway and Milner [6], which emphasized the important relationship between fiscal adjustment and sustainable trade liberalization. Subsequent work has established a strategy for realizing the efficiency gains from tariff reform without reducing public revenue for a small economy through the combination of a cut in import duties and an increase in domestic consumption taxes [8]. Developing countries (low- and middle-income countries) in particular experience declining tax revenues due to falling income and trade tax revenues [9]. This is why developing countries need to develop alternative sources of revenue to replace losses of trade tax revenue if they are to enhance trade liberalization [2].

This paper complements the literature by assessing the impact of trade liberalisation on domestic tax revenue in a least developed country (LDC) exemplified by the case of Laos. It aims to address two research questions related to tariff liberalization in Laos: has the country recovered from domestic taxes the revenues it lost from tariff liberalization over the past one and half decades? How much do indirect taxes need to be changed in response to tariff liberalization to maintain the current account deficit from deteriorating, while keep the same level of productive investment in the economy? We analyse the transition from trade liberalization to domestic taxes. We then apply a simple computable general equilibrium (CGE) model for Laos to quantify the fiscal impact of tariff liberalization.

Assessing the fiscal impact of trade liberalization in Laos can provide insights for tax reforms in LDCs. First, there is no Lao study on the optimal VAT rate given the tariff rate. International studies emphasize the need for replacing tariff with domestic taxes, especially value-added tax (VAT), but provide little guidance about what the VAT rate should be. In this paper, we argue that the VAT rate should be determined by the state of the economy given the tariff rate. Second, the net effect of tariff liberalization on government revenue is an empirical issue, which depends on the size of the tariff cut, the response of imports to the tax change, the relative importance of import tariffs as a source of public revenue, and changes in other tax bases. The detailed analysis of fiscal adjustments in a small, developing, and landlocked economy, which, furthermore, relies heavily on tariff revenue, can be of considerable help to policymakers and economists interested in trade liberalization [3].

The proposed CGE model is suitable for analysing the fiscal impact of trade liberalization in Laos for three reasons. First, it provides a simple but rigorous method to estimate the direction and magnitude of fiscal consequences based on the empirical elasticities of substitution and transformation between foreign and domestic goods [4]. The model is simple because it contains two sectors (i.e., export sector and non-traded sector) and three goods (i.e., export good, non-traded (domestic) good, and import good). The empirical elasticities are derived from the estimation of econometric models using Lao data. Second, it requires modest data, namely national income, fiscal and balance-of-payment accounts, which are normally released by the Government of Lao PDR. Third, it facilitates the interpretation of results from more complex CGE models of previous Lao studies such as Kyophilavong [10] for economic impact of mining booms and Warr [18] for poverty impact of rural road development, since these are essentially multisector analogues of the small models proposed in this paper.

The plan of the paper is as follows. Section 2 presents a short background on the Lao economy. Section 3 analyses the transition from trade liberalization to domestic taxes in Laos. Section 4 explains the structure of CGE model used for the analysis and data source. Simulation results and policy implications are presented in Section 5. Section 6 concludes the paper.

2. Background of the Lao Economy

Laos is a least-developed, natural resource-based economy. According to the 2018 triennial review[1], Laos has for the first time passed two out of three LDC graduation criteria: GNI (gross national income) per capita and Human Assets Index (HAI). GNI per capita rose from US$1,232 in 2015 to US$1,996 in 2018, which passed the graduation threshold of US$1,230. HAI increased from 60.8 in 2015 to 72.8 in 2018, which exceeded the graduation threshold of 66. The largest improvement of HAI element was adult literacy rate, followed by gross secondary enrolment ratio and under-five mortality rate. But the Economic Vulnerability Index (EVI) measuring the country's resilience to shocks and instability is still to be met. EVI improved from 36.2 in 2015 to 32.7 in 2018, which has not yet passed the graduation threshold of 32.[2] Key improvements of EVI elements include the share of agriculture in gross domestic product (GDP), victims of natural disasters, and export concentration. Limited improvements of EVI elements include agricultural instability and remoteness. Lack of improvement of EVI element was export instability. Nonetheless, if Laos sustains development gains and meets the criteria again in 2021, it will be formally removed from the list of LDCs in 2024.

Over the period 2011-2015, Laos has achieved rapid economic growth, but partially achieved inclusive economic growth. Growth rate of the Lao economy, measured by the annual growth of real GDP, recorded at 7.8% over the period 2011-2015, which was almost twice higher than the average growth rate of GDP (4.1%) for economies in East Asia and the Pacific over the same period. Sustaining rapid GDP growth raised the level of its real GDP per capita by 28%, increasing from US$1,216 in 2011 to US$1,557 in 2015 [24]. This is an encouraging result for utilizing economic growth as an instrument to narrow income gap across countries in the region and to fight poverty in poor countries such as Laos.

On the demand side, GDP growth in Laos has been mainly driven by growth in physical capital accumulation. Sources of GDP growth can be categorised into four factors: physical capital, education, labour input, and total factor productivity (TFP) based on the augmented Solow-growth model [14, 17].Figure 1 illustrates the contributions of the growth of each factor to the growth of real GDP for Laos and some selected Asian countries over the period 2011-2015. It shows that the growth rate of physical capital accounted for 62% of GDP growth in Laos, which was higher than other Asian countries such as Vietnam, China, Thailand, and Republic of Korea. In contrast, education was the smallest contributor to growth in Laos, which accounted for only 6% of GDP growth.

---

[1] Conducted by the Committee for Development Policy, United Nations Economic and Social Council.

[2] Lower EVI index means better country's economic development.

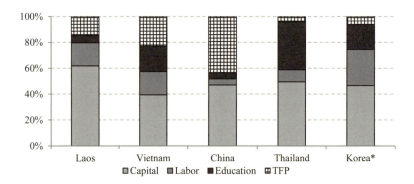

Figure 1. Sources of GDP Growth for Laos and Selected Asian Countries, 2011-2015

Note: * Republic of Korea. TFP stands for total factor productivity.

Source: Author's calculation using data from [24].

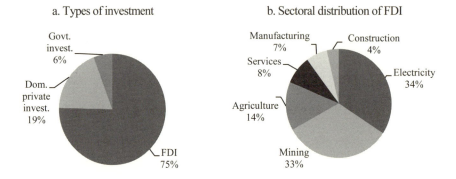

Figure 2. Types of Investment and Distribution of FDI by Sector in Laos, 2011-2015

Note: 'Govt. invest.' stands for 'government investment'. 'Dom. Private invest.' stands for 'domestic private investment.

Data on types of investment and sectoral distribution of FDI are based on value of approved investment projects.

Source: Authors' calculation using investment data from [15].

The growth in physical capital accumulation has been driven by foreign direct investment (FDI) inflows. Figure 2a shows the proportion of three types of investment in Laos during 2011-2015: FDI, domestic private investment, and government investment. FDI accounted for 75% of total investment, while domestic private investment accounted for only 19% of total investment (Figure 2a). About two thirds of FDI inflows concentrated in electricity and mining sectors (Figure 2b). It is still unclear whether rapid economic growth driven by FDI in Laos has resulted in the diversification of economic activities and generated sufficiently large number of jobs in the country.

On the production side, the service and electricity sectors have increasingly become the key driver of economic growth in Laos. The share of services in GDP increased from 36% in 2011 to 41% in 2015, while the share of electricity in GDP increased from 4% to 7% over the same period. Meanwhile, the share of agriculture and forestry in GDP reduced from 27% to 17% in the same period. The shares of manufacturing and construction in GDP remain unchanged or slightly decreased (Figure 3). According to the World Bank [23], the expansion of services has been resulted from the liberalization of trade, tourism, banking, and transport sectors, and spillovers from natural resource projects.

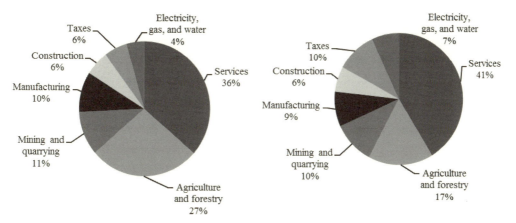

Figure 3. Sectoral Distribution of GDP in Laos (%), 2011 and 2015
Source: Data for 2011 were obtained from [13]. Data for 2015 were obtained from [1].

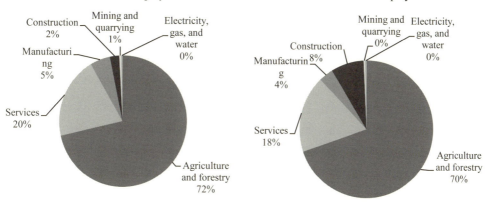

Figure 4. Sectoral Distribution of Employment in Laos, 2010 and 2015
Source: Authors' calculation using data from [11, 12].

Significant changes in the structure of outputs have been associated with limited changes in the structure of employment for the period 2010-2015. The analysis of outputs in Figure 3 and employment in Figure 4 reveals three salient features of structural change in the Lao economy.

- Increased share of services in GDP was not associated with greater share of employment within the sector. The share of employment in the service sector fell from 20% of total employment in

2010 to 18% in 2015 (Figure 4). This may reflect productivity improvement in services, which could produce more outputs without hiring additional labours. Further expansion of the service sector is needed to absorb additional labour force.

- The agriculture and forestry sector has been characterized by low productivity. The share of employment in agriculture and forestry sector accounted for 70% in 2015 (Figure 4b), but it could generate real output for only 17% of GDP (Figure 3b). This confirms the need for improving productivity and promoting investment in manufacturing and service sectors to absorb surplus labour in agriculture. Employment in the manufacturing sector, for instance, accounted for only 4% of total employment, but its real output accounted for 9% of GDP.
- The construction sector has become one of the key sectors for generating jobs. The share of employment in the construction sector rose from 2% in 2010 to 8% in 2015 (Figure 4) although the share of its real output in GDP remained unchanged (Figure 3).

The status of LDC and limited diversification in the Lao economy indicate that Laos has not reached a development threshold where it can rely more on sophisticated tax instruments. It has weak tax administrations, as well as large informal sectors (with unrecorded or illicit transactions), narrowing the tax base. We analyse how Laos managed to transition from tariff to domestic taxes over the past one and half decades in the next section.

3. Transition from Tariff to Domestic Taxes in Laos

Three main trends can be identified in the evolution of trade liberalization in Laos since 2000. First, Laos has reduced tariff rates since 2000 when it has deepened economic integration into regional economy through full member of the ASEAN Economic Community and the global economy through the formal accession to the WTO in 2013. These agreements entailed profound changes to Laos' regulatory framework governing international trade, including tariff and non-tariff measures (NTMs). Figure 5 shows the evolution of the weighted average applied tariff rate in Laos for import of goods from all trading partners, Thailand, China and France from 2000 to 2017. It reveals two salient features of tariff liberalization. First, Laos' applied tariff rate for all trading partners shows a downward trend, falling from 14.06% in 2000 to 5.22% in 2014 and 1.48% in 2017. Second, ASEAN members face lower tariff rate than non-ASEAN members. From 2000 to 2017, the tariff rate faced by ASEAN member such as Thailand and member of ASEAN-China FTA such as China reduced by more than 10 percentage points, while that faced by non-ASEAN member such as France fell by only four percentage points.

Parallel to tariff liberalization is the reduction of NTMs on Laos' imports since its WTO accession. According to World Bank [21], the percentage of products covered by at least one NTM reduced from 72% in 2011 to 13% in 2014. A notable reduction in NTMs is the use of quantity controls. Yet, the frequency of using quantity controls in Laos is still higher than other regional countries, such as Indonesia and the Philippines. A similar trend of NTMs reduction in Laos can be observed in the case of the coverage ratio where the reduction goes from 83% to 42% of the import value that is subjected to at least one NTM. The number of NTMs that are applied to the average import product (pervasiveness score) was also significantly reduced from 2.6 in 2011 to 0.4 in 2014.

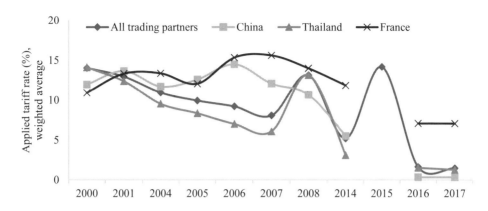

Figure 5. Reduction of Laos' Tariff Rate, by Trading Partners
Source: Authors' calculation using data from World Bank's World Integrated Trade Solution.

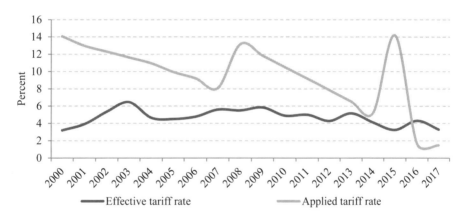

Figure 6. Effective and Applied Tariff Rates in Laos, 2000-2017
Source: Authors' calculation using applied tariff rate from World Bank's World Integrated Trade Solution and effective tariff rate from [1].

Second, the effective tariff rate measured as the ratio of import duties to total import of goods is lower than the applied tariff rate between 2000 and 2015 (Figure 6). The effective tariff rate showed a stable trend, while the applied tariff rate showed a downward trend but was consistently higher than the applied tariff rate. Hence, the gap between the effective and applied tariff rates reduced from 10.87 percentage points in 2000 to 1.12 percentage points in 2014 and increased to 10.94% in 2015. Such gap can be explained by three factors: exemptions on imports of raw materials for the manufacture of exports; exemptions for imports by government and donor-funded projects; and concessional duty rates of only 1% on imports of plant, equipment and raw materials by approved domestic and foreign investors [5].

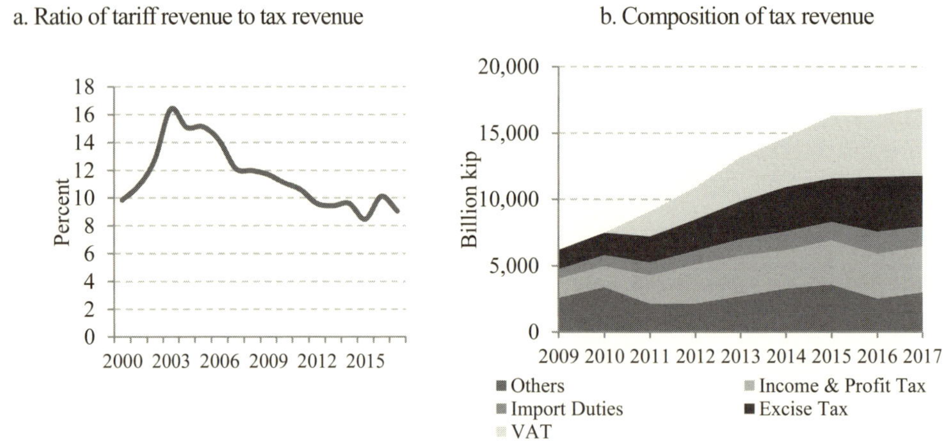

a. Ratio of tariff revenue to tax revenue

b. Composition of tax revenue

Figure 7. Tariff Revenue Reduction and Alternative Sources of Tax Revenue

Source: Authors' calculation using data from [1].

Third, loss in tariff revenue is compensated by raising revenues from domestic taxes, especially through the introduction of value-added tax (VAT). For a period of 14 years, the ratio of tariff revenue to tax revenue dropped by almost half from 16.38% in 2003 to 9.04% in 2017 (Figure 7a). Among domestic taxes, VAT is the most important sources of tax revenue. VAT was introduced in 2010 at a rate of 10%. The ratio of VAT revenue to tax revenue rose from 21% in 2011 to 25% in 2014 and 30% in 2017 (Figure 7b). However, VAT revenue collection is not very effective. In 2011, the ratio of VAT revenue to GDP was only 2.92%, which was only one-third of the official VAT rate. In 2017, the ratio of VAT revenue to GDP increased slightly to 3.66%, which was still far below the VAT rate (not reported in Figure 7). A possible explanation for this is the limited capacity of government agency to collect tax from companies across the country [25]. The Revenue Collection Division in the Tax Department is tasked to monitor the compliance of large taxpayers, and currently oversees more 500 companies in Laos. The top 10 taxpayers represent 66% of total large business tax collection in 2017, and the top 50 taxpayers represent almost 90% of total large business tax collection.

4. CGE Modelling and Data

This section constructs a CGE model for explaining the relationship between tariff revenue, domestic taxes, and other macroeconomic variables. The CGE model is calibrated with Lao macroeconomic data.

4.1 CGE Modelling

This paper applies the 1-2-3 CGE model to explore the impact of tariff reduction on public revenue in Laos [3, 4]. The basic nature of the 1-2-3 CGE model is a modified Salter-Swan methodology which separates the economy into two producing sectors and three goods. The country is small in world markets, facing fixed world prices for exports and imports. The economy consists of two sectors of production, one for export good and another for domestic good. Three goods include an export good (denoted as E), a domestic good (D), and an import (M). Export good is sold to foreigners and is not demanded domestically. Domestic good is only sold domestically. Both export and domestic goods are produced in the country. Import good is produced in foreign country.

The CGE model is presented in Table 1. It consists of 20 equations, two identities, and 19 endogenous variables. The model has three actors: a producer, a household, a government and the rest of the world. Equation (1) defines the domestic production possibility frontier, which gives the maximum achievable combinations of E and D that the economy can supply. The function is assumed to be concave and will be specified as a constant elasticity of transformation (CET) function with transformation elasticity Ω. The constant $\bar{X}$ defines aggregate production and is fixed. Equation (4) gives the efficient ratio of exports to domestic output (E/D) as a function of relative prices. Equation (9) defines the price of the composite commodity and is the cost-function dual to the first-order condition underlying equation (4). The composite good price P^x corresponds to the GDP deflator.

Equation (2) defines a composite commodity made up of D and M which is consumed by the single consumer. The composite commodity is given by a constant elasticity of substitution (CES) aggregation function of M and D, with substitution elasticity σ. Consumers maximize utility, which is equivalent to maximizing Q in this model, and equation (5) gives the desired ratio of M to D as a function of relative price. Equation (14) defines the price of the composite commodity. It is the cost-function dual to the first-order conditions underlying equation (5). The price P^q corresponds to an aggregate consumer price. Equation (7) determines household income. Equation (3) defines household demand for the composite good.

In Table 1, the price equations define relationships among seven prices. There are fixed world prices for E and M, domestic prices for E and M, the price of the domestic good D; and prices for the two composite commodities, X and Q. Equations (1) and (2) are linearly homogeneous, as are the corresponding dual price equations, (13) and (14). Equations (4) and (5) are homogeneous of degree zero in prices - doubling all prices, for example, leaves real demand and the desired export and import ratios unchanged. Since only relative prices matter, it is necessary to define a numeraire price; in equation (15), this is specified to be the exchange rate R.

Equations (16) ~ (18) define the market-clearing equilibrium conditions. Supply must equal demand for D and Q, and the balance of trade constraint must be satisfied. Equation (19) defines investment equal to saving. Equation (20) defines the budget balance. The two identities - (21) and (22) - arise from the homogeneity assumptions.

Table 1. CGE Model with Taxation

Real Flows

(1) $\bar{X} = \alpha(\lambda E^\gamma + (1-\lambda)D^\gamma)^{\frac{1}{\gamma}}$

(2) $Q^S = \epsilon(\delta M^{-\rho} + (1-\delta)D^{-\rho})^{-\frac{1}{\rho}}$

(3) $Q^D = C + Z + \bar{G}$

(4) $\frac{E}{D} = k\left(\frac{P^e}{P^d}\right)^\Omega$

(5) $\frac{M}{D} = k'\left(\frac{P^t}{P^m}\right)^\sigma$

Nominal Flows

(6) $T = t^m \cdot R \cdot pw^m \cdot M + t^s \cdot P^q \cdot Q^D$
$\quad + t^y \cdot Y - t^e \cdot R \cdot pw^e \cdot E$

(7) $Y = P^x \cdot \bar{X} + tr \cdot P^q + re \cdot R$

(8) $S = \bar{s} \cdot Y + R \cdot \bar{B} + S^g$

(9) $C \cdot P^t = (1 - \bar{s} - t^y) \cdot Y$

(10) $P^m = (1 + t^m) \cdot R \cdot pw^m$

(11) $P^e = (1 + t^e) \cdot R \cdot pw^e$

(12) $P^t = (1 + t^s) \cdot P^q$

(13) $P^x = \frac{P^e \cdot E + P^d \cdot D}{\bar{X}}$

(14) $P^q = \frac{P^m \cdot M + P^d \cdot D}{Q}$

(15) $R = 1$

Equilibrium Conditions

(16) $D^D - D^S = 0$

(17) $Q^D - Q^S = 0$

(18) $pw^m \cdot M - pw^e \cdot E - ft - re = \bar{B}$

(19) $P^t \cdot Z - S = 0$

(20) $T - P^q \cdot \bar{G} - tr \cdot P^q - ft \cdot R - S^g = 0$

Accounting Identities

(21) $P^x \cdot \bar{X} = P^e \cdot E + P^d \cdot D^S$

(22) $P^q \cdot Q^S = P^m \cdot M + P^d \cdot D^D$

Endogenous variables:
E: Export good
D: Domestic good
M: Import good
D^S: Supply of domestic good
D^D: Demand for domestic good
Q^S: Supply of composite good
Q^D: Demand for composite good
P^e: Domestic price of export good
P^m: Domestic price of import good
P^d: Producer price of domestic good
P^t: Sales price of composite good
P^x: Price of aggregate output
P^q: Price of composite good
R: Exchange rate
T: Tax revenue
S^g: Government savings
Y: Total income
C: Aggregate consumption
S: Aggregate savings
Z: Aggregate real investment

Exogenous variables:
pw^m: World price of import good

Exogenous variables (continue):
pw^e: World price of export good
t^m: Tariff rate
t^e: Export subsidy rate
t^s: Sales/excise/value-added tax rate
t^y: Direct tax rate
tr: Government transfers
ft: Foreign transfers to government
re: Foreign remittances to private sector
$\bar{s}$: Average savings rate
$\bar{X}$: Aggregate output
$\bar{G}$: Real government demand
$\bar{B}$: Balance of trade
Ω: Export transformation elasticity, $\Omega = 1/(\rho - 1)$
σ: Import substitution elasticity, $\sigma = 1/(1 - \rho)$

Parameters:
α: Shift parameter of CES
λ: Share parameter of CES
ϵ: Shift parameter of CET
δ: Share parameter of CET
γ: Substitution parameter of CES
ρ: Substitution parameter of CET

Note: k is defined as $\left(\frac{1-\lambda}{\lambda}\right)^\Omega$. k' is defined as $\left(\frac{1-\delta}{\delta}\right)^\sigma$.

Source: Authors' construction from [3, 4].

4.2 Data and Calibration

To conduct simulations in the CGE model, we used the 2016 data for national income, fiscal, and balance-of-payments accounts from the 2017 Annual Economic Report published by the Bank of the Lao PDR (Table A.1). The original data were measured in billions of kip (LAK). In the calibration, all data were scaled and indexed with respect to output, which is set to 1.00 in the base year.

Empirical estimates of elasticities for CES and CET were obtained from Devarajan [4]. The estimate of elasticity for CES for Laos is 0.84. Since the estimate of elasticity for CET for Laos is not available, it is proxy by that of Myanmar which is 0.24. We then used these elasticities and macroeconomic data to calibrate other parameters (Table A.2) and variables of the CGE (Table A.3).

5. Simulation Results and Policy Implications

In this section, we measure the impact of tariff liberalization on government revenue and welfare in Laos, given various changes to the effective tariff and indirect tax rates. Government revenue captures direct impact of tariff liberalization. Welfare effects of tariff liberalization are measured by private consumption and total investment (public and private), which capture indirect impact of tariff liberalization. The purpose of this simulation is to illustrate whether the target policy variables of tariff and tax reform should consider both government revenue and welfare indicators; and how different combinations of effective tariff and indirect tax rates result in different economic outcomes. Devarajan [3, 4] have used this approach to simulate trade reforms for developing countries.

5.1 Simulation Results

Using the CGE model developed in Section 4, we simulate three policy scenarios based on changes in effective tariff and indirect tax rates: (i) fully coordinated tariff and tax reform; (ii) moderately coordinated tariff and tax reform; and (iii) lack of coordinated tariff and tax reform. Table 2 summarizes key policy instruments and their changes in three policy scenarios. In each policy scenario, policy instruments change in four steps from the baseline: 20%, 50%, 80%, and 100%.

The fully coordinated tariff and tax reform consists of two instruments, namely tariff rate (exogenous) and endogenous indirect tax rate, which aim to maximize private consumption and maintain the same level of investment. The salient feature of the first policy scenario is that indirect tax rate is determined by the tariff rate and the state of the economy. Changes in government revenue depend on tariff reduction and optimal indirect tax rate. This implies the customs authorities design the tariff rates set out in free trade agreements (FTA) and then consult them with the tax authorities to determined appropriate indirect tax rate based on the state of the economy. The coordination between customs and tax authorities is likely to happen in Laos, where both the Customs and Tax Departments are operating under the Ministry of Finance. But determining appropriate indirect tax rate remains the key challenge given limited research capacity and prevalence of informal economy in the form of micro and small enterprises.

Table 2. Policy Scenarios for Coordinated Tariff and Tax Reform

Policy scenarios	Policy instruments	Changes in policy instruments			
		± 20%	± 50%	± 80%	± 100%
1. Fully coordinated tariff and tax reform	1. Tariff rate (tm) 2. Endogenous indirect tax rate (ts)	tm (-20%)	tm (-50%)	tm (-80%)	tm (-100%)
2. Moderately coordinated tariff and tax reform	1. Tariff rate (tm) 2. Indirect tax rate (ts)	tm (-20%) ts (+20%)	tm (-50%) ts (+50%)	tm (-80%) ts (+80%)	tm (-100%) ts (+100%)
3. Uncoordinated tariff and tax reform	Tariff rate (tm)	tm (-20%)	tm (-50%)	tm (-80%)	tm (-100%)

Note: '-' denotes 'decrease'. '+' denotes 'increase'.

Source: Authors' construction.

The second policy scenario is the moderately coordinated tariff and tax reform, which consists of two policy instruments, namely tariff rate and indirect tax rate. It aims to maximize private consumption regardless of the level of investment. The salient feature of the second policy scenario is that both tariff and indirect tax rates are determined exogenously and decreases in tariff rates correspond to increases in indirect tax rates. Changes in government revenue depend on the net effect of tariff reduction and indirect tax increase. This may reflect the current form of tariff and tax reform in Laos, which aims to replace losses in trade taxes with domestic taxes.

The third policy scenario is the lack of coordinated tax reform, which considers only tariff rate as the key policy instrument. It aims to maximize private consumption regardless of the level of investment. The salient feature of the third policy scenario is that tariff reform is implemented without domestic tax reform. Changes in government revenue only depend on tariff reduction. It reflects the delay in designing indirect tax rates in response to tariff reduction under ASEAN+1 FTAs, Regional Comprehensive Economic Partnership (RCEP), and World Trade Organization (WTO).

Scenario 1: fully coordinated tariff and tax reform. In Scenario 1, we conduct the simulations in two steps. First, the current effective indirect tax rate is assessed whether it is optimal given the current VAT rate. Our simulation result shows that the current effective indirect tax rate is higher than its optimal rate. Column 2 of Table 3 shows that the indirect tax rate should be reduced by 21% from 6.2% (current indirect tax rate) to 4.9% (optimal indirect tax rate). Indirect tax reduction will decrease sales price by 1.21%. This will stimulate private consumption by 1.27%, while reducing tax revenue by 10.82% and government saving by 174%.

Second, we simulate the impact of tariff reductions on indirect tax and other economic variables. Our simulation results show that the coordinated tariff and tax reform for Laos means lower government revenue through the reduction of the combination of tariff and indirect tax rates. Columns 3-6 of Table 3 show different estimates of the indirect tax rate associated with tariff reductions. The reduction of tariff rate by 20% requires the actual indirect tax rate to reduce by 16%. Further reduction of tariff rate from 50% to the elimination of tariff rate (reduced by 100% of baseline) requires lower reduction of the actual indirect tax rate ranging from 10.9% to 2.3%.

Lower indirect tax rates associated with tariff liberalization will stimulate consumption and production in the economy. The reduction of tariff rate by 20% reduces prices of goods and services in the economy. The notable declines in prices are sales price and import price, which will drop by 1.50% and 0.64%, respectively. Lower sales price and import price stimulate private consumption by 1.14% and reduce nominal income by 0.38%. Meanwhile, the reduction of both tariff and indirect tax rates will reduce government revenue by 10.94% and government saving by 170%. The worsening tax revenue loss reflects largely the non-optimal indirect tax rate, which needs to be reduced in parallel with tariff liberalization.

Table 3. Fully Coordinated Tariff and Tax Reform in the Lao Economy

Variable	% change of baseline				
Changes in policy instrument					
Effective Tariff Rate (tm)	0.00	-20.00	-50.00	-80.00	-100.00
Responses of endogenous variables					
Target variables					
Consumption (Cn)	1.27	1.14	1.14	1.14	1.14
Investment (Z)	0.00	0.00	0.00	0.00	0.00
Tax Revenue (TAX)	-10.82	-10.94	-12.32	-13.70	-14.62
Indirect Tax Rate (ts)	-20.83	-15.99	-10.94	-5.80	-2.29
Other important variables					
Total Income (Y)	0.00	-0.38	-0.95	-1.53	-1.91
Aggregate Savings (S)	-4.39	-4.44	-4.99	-5.55	-5.91
Government Savings (Sg)	-173.81	-170.06	-183.66	-197.26	-206.22
Adjustment of prices and exchange rate					
Import Price (Pm)	0.00	-0.64	-1.61	-2.58	-3.22
Export Price (Pe)	0.00	0.00	0.00	0.00	0.00
Sales Price (Pt)	-1.21	-1.50	-2.07	-2.64	-3.02
Price of Supply (Pq)	0.00	-0.58	-1.44	-2.31	-2.89
Price of Output (Px)	0.00	-0.36	-0.91	-1.45	-1.82
Price of Domestic Good (Pd)	0.00	-0.53	-1.32	-2.12	-2.65
Exchange Rate (Er)	0.00	0.00	0.00	0.00	0.00

Source: Authors' calculation based on CGE simulation.

Scenario 2: partially coordinated tariff and tax reform. Scenario 2 involves reductions in tariff rates and increases in indirect tax rates by 20%, 50%, 80%, and 100% (first panel of Table 4). The combination of 20% reduction in tariff rate and 20% increase in indirect tax rate will raise sales price by 0.59%, while reducing prices of import, supply, domestic good, and output by 0.64%, 0.58%, 0.53%, and 0.36%, respectively. The net effect of price changes reduces private consumption by 0.96% and nominal income by 0.38%, while raises tax revenue by 7.64% and investment by 6.03%. Higher tax revenue will increase government saving by 128% and aggregate saving by 3.11%. The combinations of further reductions in tariff rates and further increases in indirect tax rates worsen private consumption and nominal income, but increase tax revenue and investment (second panel of Table 4).

Scenario 3: uncoordinated tariff and tax reform. Scenario 3 involves reductions in tariff rates by 20%, 50%, 80%, and 100%, given the indirect tax rate (first panel of Table 5). The 20% reduction in tariff rate will reduce prices of goods and services in the economy (column 1 of Table 5). The notable reductions of prices are import price (0.64%) and sale price (0.58%). The net effect of price changes increases private consumption by 0.20% and investment by 2.55%, while reduces tax revenue by 2.69%. Lower tax revenue will reduce government saving by 37% and aggregate saving by 1.1%. Further reductions in tariff rates stimulate private consumption and investment, but reduce tax revenue, nominal income, government saving and aggregate saving (columns 3~6 of Table 5).

Table 4. Partially Coordinated Tariff and Tax Reform in the Lao Economy

Variable	% change of baseline			
Changes in policy instruments				
Effective Tariff Rate (tm)	−20.00	−50.00	−80.00	−100.00
Effective Indirect Tax Rate (ts)	+20.00	+50.00	+80.00	+100.00
Responses of endogenous variables				
Target variables				
Consumption (Cn)	−0.96	−2.42	−3.68	−4.55
Investment (Z)	6.03	9.62	13.03	15.38
Tax Revenue (TAX)	7.64	18.87	29.82	36.28
Other important variables				
Total Income (Y)	−0.38	−0.95	−1.53	−1.91
Aggregate Savings (S)	3.11	7.64	12.14	14.73
Government Savings (Sg)	128.39	315.82	502.07	610.11
Adjustment of prices and exchange rate				
Import Price (Pm)	−0.64	−1.61	−2.58	−3.22
Export Price (Pe)	0.00	0.00	0.00	0.00
Sales Price (Pt)	0.59	1.52	2.24	2.77
Price of Supply (Pq)	−0.58	−1.44	−2.31	−2.89
Price of Output (Px)	−0.36	−0.91	−1.45	−1.82
Price of Domestic Good (Pd)	−0.53	−1.32	−2.12	−2.65
Exchange Rate (Er)	0.00	0.00	0.00	0.00

Source: Authors' calculation based on CGE simulation.

Table 5. Uncoordinated Tariff and Tax Reform

Variable	% change of baseline			
Changes in policy instruments				
Effective Tariff Rate (tm)	-20.00	-50.00	-80.00	-100.00
Responses of endogenous variables				
Target variables				
Consumption (Cn)	0.20	0.50	0.80	1.01
Investment (Z)	2.55	1.74	0.92	0.36
Tax Revenue (TAX)	-2.69	-6.72	-10.76	-13.46
Other important variables				
Total Income (Y)	-0.38	-0.95	-1.53	-1.91
Aggregate Savings (S)	-1.09	-2.72	-4.35	-5.44
Government Savings (Sg)	-37.43	-93.67	-150.01	-187.63
Adjustment of prices and exchange rate				
Import Price (Pm)	-0.64	-1.61	-2.58	-3.22
Export Price (Pe)	0.00	0.00	0.00	0.00
Sales Price (Pt)	-0.58	-1.44	-2.31	-2.89
Price of Supply (Pq)	-0.58	-1.44	-2.31	-2.89
Price of Output (Px)	-0.36	-0.91	-1.45	-1.82
Price of Domestic Good (Pd)	-0.53	-1.32	-2.12	-2.65
Exchange Rate (Er)	0.00	0.00	0.00	0.00

Source: Authors' calculation based on CGE simulation.

5.2 Policy Implications

The key result of this paper—the greater the coordinated tariff and tax reform, the greater the private consumption gains to Lao people—is a key policy implication for further trade liberalisation between Laos and its trading partners. Our simulation results indicate that the coordinated tariff and tax reform for Laos means lower government revenue through the reduction of the combination of tariff and indirect tax rates. Any policy designed for raising tax revenue should aim at improving tax collection system and broadening tax base rather raising the indirect tax rate. In the short run, however, while both tariff and indirect tax reductions expand private consumption, they reduce tariff revenue, leading to a lower level of tax revenue in the more aggressive cases of tariff and indirect tax reductions.

The worsening tax revenue loss reflects largely the non-optimal indirect tax rate, which needs to be reduced in parallel with tariff liberalization. This is likely to be a temporary phenomenon given the country's current stage of economic development. Over time, such optimal indirect tax rate coupled with cheaper imported intermediate and capital goods will help to build domestic productive capacity, which will likely broaden domestic tax base. That said, the turnaround will also depend on the country's ability to improve business environment and productivity of enterprises. Laos is ranked 141 out of 190 economies according to the World Bank's ease of doing business index in 2018[3], behind all the other economies in the region, except Myanmar.

Strengthening the tax collection system under the optimal indirect tax rate will improve fair business competition in the Lao economy. Law-abiding enterprises find competition with non-registered and tax-evading enterprises unfair and detrimental to their own businesses. The proportion of registered enterprises that reported informal competitors' practices related to non-compliance of tax payment was largest for small enterprises (27.3%), followed by medium enterprises (22.7%) and large enterprises (12.5%). About 77% of registered enterprises are competing with unregistered enterprises [22]. Concern about informal competitors' practices tends to rise in the future because non-registered enterprises have been growing alongside registered enterprises. According to World Bank [19], household-based enterprises, a proxy variable for non-registered enterprises, increased by almost 50% between 1997/98 and 2002/03. Household-based enterprises perceived registration procedures as particularly burdensome; and the benefits of registering do not seem to offset the costs of moving to formal sector.

Improving the efficiency of import system through non-tariff measure reform will lower the cost of doing business in Laos. The current import licensing scheme and the associated fees increase significantly the cost of importing, for three main reasons [21]. First, the system for granting licences is centralised in the capital, resulting in increased costs for rural traders. Second, the lack of coordination between central authorities in charge of granting licences and border agencies in charge of enforcing the licences leaves room for discretion for provincial authorities to influence the process. Third, internal procedures for granting licences by the central government are not well communicated to the trading community, leaving room for unnecessary delays and encouraging informal payments to expedite the process. These extra trade costs are passed onto the price faced by consumers in sectors such as vegetable oils, processed foods, and vegetables, with negative implications for households, especially the poor; and they encourage importers to resort to informal channels to bring their products to the market, putting the health of consumers at risk.

Developing sector-specific workforce in line with potential export-oriented industry will raise productivity of enterprises, which has been stagnant over the past decade. The actual level of total factor productivity (TFP) was estimated to be about half of the potential level of TFP and lower than countries with similar level of per capita income. The actual labour productivity, measured by value added per worker, was US$ 1,600 per worker which was about three times lower than the potential labour productivity of US$ 5,300 per worker. Similarly, the actual capital intensity of the median enterprises, measured by the book value of capital divided by the number of workers, was US$ 2,400 per worker, which was about double lower than the potential capital intensity of US$ 4,400 per worker [20].

6. Conclusions

Trade policy in Laos has changed significantly since 2000. Being a member of ASEAN Economic Community, ASEAN+1 FTAs, and WTO have contributed to reductions of tariff and non-tariff

---

[3] See: http://www.doingbusiness.org/content/dam/doingBusiness/media/Annual-Reports/English/DB2018-Full-Report.pdf.

measures. The analysis of the transition from trade liberalization to domestic taxes reveals that Laos has been able to recover from domestic taxes the revenues it lost from tariff reduction over the past one and half decades. First, there is a robust sign of strong replacement of the tariff revenue loss through VAT. VAT generated LAK 5,510 billion or 30% of tax revenue in 2017, which was about twice higher than the ratio of tariff revenue to tax revenue in 2000. Second, tariff rate faced by all trading partners reduced by more than tenfold from 14.06% in 2000 to 1.48% in 2017, while ASEAN countries faced lower Laos' tariff rate than non-ASEAN countries. Third, the effective tariff rate is relatively low due to exemptions on imports of raw materials, capital goods and government procurements.

The simulation results of tariff liberalization using a CGE model reveals that private consumption gains are largest when tariff reform is well coordinated with indirect tax reform. The coordinated tariff and tax reform treats an indirect tax rate as an endogenous variable, which is determined by the state of the economy given the tariff rate. In this policy scenario, our simulation results show that reduction in tariff rate results in lower effective indirect tax rate. In particular, the 20% tariff reduction will increase private consumption by 1.14%, but will decrease the effective indirect tax rate from 6.2% to 5.2% and will reduce tax revenue by 11%. The worsening tax revenue loss reflects the non-optimal indirect tax rate, which needs to be reduced by 11%. In other words, high domestic tax rate has increased domestic tax revenue, which significantly exceeded revenue loss from tariff reduction.

The key result of this paper—the greater the coordinated tariff and tax reform, the greater the private consumption gains to Lao people—is a key policy implication for further trade liberalisation in Laos. Our simulation results indicate that the coordinated tariff and tax reform means lower government revenue through the reduction of the combination of tariff and indirect tax rates. Any policy designed for raising tax revenue should aim at improving tax collection system and broadening tax base rather raising the indirect tax rate.

Appendix

Table A. 1. Laos' Macroeconomic Data in 2016 for CGE Simulations

		LAK Billion	Output=1			LAK Billion	Output=1
	National Accounts			3	**Fiscal Account**		
1	Output (Value Added)	114589.72	1.00		Revenue	19363.81	0.17
	Wages	31416.58	0.27		Non-Tax	2976.63	0.03
					Current Expenditure	18637.00	0.16
	GDP at market prices	129528.72	1.13		Goods & Services	14215.00	0.12
	Private Consumption	92474.21	0.81		Interest Payments	1585.00	0.01
	Public Consumption	15484.34	0.14		Transfers & Subsidies	2837.00	0.02
	Investment	34228.12	0.30		Capital Expenditure	7818.00	0.07
	Exports	35886.17	0.31		Fiscal Balance	-7091.19	-0.06
	Imports	54382.42	0.47				
	Tax Revenue			4	**Balance of Payments**		
2	Sales & Excise Tax	8344.00	0.07		Exports - Imports	-18496.25	-0.16
	Import Tariffs	1810.00	0.02		Net Profits & Dividends	-3171.49	-0.03
	Export Duties	49.45	0.00		Interest Payments	-3212.46	-0.03
	Others	2547.55	0.02		Net Private Transfers	1589.84	0.01
	Personal Income Tax	1470.00	0.01		Net Official Transfers	1753.74	0.02
	Turnover Tax	1847.00	0.02		Current Account Balance	-15595.20	-0.14
	Total	16068.00	0.14				
					External Debt	63243.41	0.55
					Debt Service Payments	2247.25	0.02

Source: Authors' compilation using data from Bank of the Lao PDR's 2017 Annual Economic Report.

Table A. 2. Calibrated Parameters

Parameters	value
Elasticity for CET (st)	0.24
Elasticity for CES/Q (sq)	0.84
Scale for CET (at)	2.57
Share for CET (bt)	0.96
Rho for CET (rt)	5.17
Scale for CES/Q (aq)	1.97
Share for CES/Q (bq)	0.40
Rho for CES/Q (rq)	0.19

Source: Authors' calculation.

Table A.3. Calibrated Variables

Exogenous Variables	Base Year	Endogenous Variables	Base Year
World Price of Imports (wm)	0.97	Export Good (E)	0.31
World Price of Exports (we)	1.00	Import Good (M)	0.49
		Supply of Domestic Good (Ds)	0.69
Import Tariffs (tm)	0.03	Demand of Domestic Good (Dd)	0.69
Export Duties (te)	0.00	Supply of Composite Good (Qs)	1.18
Indirect Taxes (ts)	0.06	Demand of Composite Good (Qd)	1.18
Direct Taxes (ty)	0.05		
		Tax Revenue (TAX)	0.14
Savings rate (sy)	0.12	Total Income (Y)	0.97
Govt. Consumption (G)	0.13	Aggregate Savings (S)	0.31
Govt. Transfers (tr)	0.01	Consumption (Cn)	0.76
Foreign Grants (ft)	0.02		
Net Priv Remittances (re)	-0.04	Import Price (Pm)	1.00
Foreign Saving (B)	0.19	Export Price (Pe)	1.00
Output (X)	1.00	Sales Price (Pt)	1.06
		Price of Supply (Pq)	1.00
		Price of Output (Px)	1.00
		Price of Dom. Good (Pd)	1.00
		Exchange Rate (Er)	1.00
		Investment (Z)	0.28
		Government Savings (Sg)	0.01
		Walras Law (Z-S)	-0.01

Source: Authors' calculation.

References

[1] Bank of Lao PDR (various issues). Annual Economic Report, Vientiane.

[2] Baunsgaard, T. and Keen, M., 2010. Tax revenue and (or?) trade liberalization. *Journal of Public Economics*, 94, pp.563–577.

[3] Devarajan, S. et al., 1997. Simple General Equilibrium Modelling. In J. F. Francois and K. A. Reinert, eds. *Applied Methods for Trade Policy Analysis*. Cambridge: Cambridge University Press, pp. 156–186.

[4] Devarajan, S., Go, D.S. and Li, H., 1999. *Quantifying the fiscal effects of trade reform*, Policy Research Working Paper No. WPS2162, Washington D.C.: World Bank.

[5] Fane, G., 2006. Trade liberalization, economic reform and poverty reduction in Lao PDR. *Journal of the Asia Pacific Economy*, 11(2), pp.213–226.

[6] Greenaway, D. and Milner, C., 1991. Fiscal dependence on trade taxes and trade policy reform. *Journal of Development Studies*, 27(3), pp.95–132.

[7] Greenaway, D., Morgan, W. and Wright, P., 2002. Trade liberalisation and growth in developing countries. *Journal of Development Economics*, 67(1), pp.229–244.

[8] Keen, M. and Ligthart, J.E., 2002. Coordinating tariff reduction and domestic tax reform. *Journal of International Economics*, 56, pp.489–507.

[9] Khattry, B. and Mohan Rao, J., 2002. Fiscal faux pas?.: an analysis of the revenue implications of trade liberalization. *World Development*, 30(8), pp.1431–1444.

[10] Kyophilavong, P., 2016. Mining booms and growth in Laos – empirical result from CGE model. *International Journal of Development Issues*, 15(1), pp.51–61.

[11] Lao Statistics Bureau, 2010. *Labour Force and Using Child Labour Survey 2010*, Vientiane.

[12] Lao Statistics Bureau, 2015. *Laos Population and Housing Census 2015*, Vientiane.

[13] Lao Statistics Bureau, 2012. *Statistical Year Book 2012*. Vientiane Capital: Ministry of Planning and Investment.

[14] Lee, J.-W. and Hong, K., 2012. Economic growth in Asia: Determinants and prospects. *Japan and the World Economy*, 24(2), pp.101–113.

[15] Ministry of Planning and Investment, 2017. *Statistics*. Available at: http://www.investlaos.gov.la/index.php/resources/statistics [Accessed November 8, 2017].

[16] Mitra, P., 1992. The coordinated reform of tariffs and indirect taxes. *The World Bank Research Observer*, 7(2), pp.195–219.

[17] Park, J., 2012. Total factor productivity growth for 12 Asian economies: The past and the future. *Japan and the World Economy*, 24(2), pp.114–127.

[18] Warr, P., 2008. How road improvement reduces poverty: the case of Laos. *Agricultural Economics*, 39(3), pp.269–279.

[19] World Bank, 2007. *Lao PDR - Private Sector and Investment Climate Assessment Reducing Investment Climate Constraints to Higher Growth*, Vientiane.

[20] World Bank, 2014. *Lao PDR Investment Climate Assessment 2014*, Vientiane.

[21] World Bank, 2016. *A Comparative Overview of the Incidence of Non-Tariff Measures on Trade in Lao PDR*, Vientiane.

[22] World Bank, 2016. *Enterprise Survey: Lao PDR 2016*. Available a t: http://documents.worldbank.org/curated/en/214641482731818886/pdf/111256-WP-PUBLIC-Lao-PDR-.pdf [Accessed November 10, 2017].

[23] World Bank, 2017. *Lao Economic Monitor: Challenges in Promoting More Inclusive Growth and Shared Prosperity*, Vientiane.

[24] World Bank, 2017. *World Development Indicators | DataBank*. Available at: http://databank.worldbank.org/data/reports.aspx?source=world-development-indicators [Accessed November 8, 2017].

[25] World Bank, 2018. *Lao PDR - Public Finance Management Modernization Program 2016-2018*, Vientiane.

Chapter 4

BUMD-tree: An Extended MD-tree using Batch Update Algorithm for Management of Moving Objects

Hiroyuki Dekihara
Hiroshima Shudo University, Faculty of Economic Sciences
1-1-1, Ozuka-higashi, Asaminami-ku, Hiroshima, Japan 731-3195

Abstract
In the fields of IoT (Internet of Things), GIS (Geographic Information System), ITS (Intelligent Transportation System), monitoring systems, and so forth, the spatial data structures for the management of moving objects are very important. Moving objects may change their attributes: location, direction, condition, etc. Therefore, the spatial data structure must manage moving objects efficiently to perform queries that search or trace the spatial data any time. However, when the data structure is updated at every unit time, the update cost will highly increase. In this paper, the new spatial data structure is proposed by extending the MD-tree which is one of the efficient spatial data structures using an update algorithm for spatial data structures managing moving objects. It is called the BUMD (the Batch Update MD) -tree. The novel concepts of the BUMD-tree are a butch insertion using a buffer array, and a simplified restructuring according to the location changes of objects. The BUMD-tree saves the update cost of the tree by using the buffer array in which reported new locations of the moving objects are stored. Moreover, the search performances of the BUMD-tree are kept although the restructuring of the tree is not performed completely.

Key Words: Spatial data structure, Moving object, Batch update, MD-tree

1. Introduction

Hierarchical data structures, such as a kd-tree[1], R-tree[2], R*-tree[3], KDB-tree[4], MD-tree[5] and so forth, have been applied for the management of spatial objects, because they provide fast algorithms to perform spatial queries. Recently, in the applications of IoT (Internet of Things), GIS (geographic Information Systems), ITS (Intelligent Transport Systems), monitoring systems, navigation systems and so forth, the moving objects should be managed efficiently to perform several functions such as a nearest neighbor query, and range queries[6]. Usually, hierarchical data structures are adopted as a spatial temporal data structure for the efficient management of moving objects, because the moving objects are treated as the special spatial data[7-11]. The main properties of moving objects are the location, velocity, direction, etc. To apply these data structures for management of moving objects, the update cost of data structure will become quite high, when objects move. In this paper, the spatial data structure using an efficient update algorithm for managing moving objects, called the BUMD (the Batch Update MD) -tree is proposed. A tree structure is one of the efficient methods of managing the objects which report their locations in a unit interval. The novel concepts of the BUMD-tree are a butch insertion using a buffer array, and the simplified restructuring according to the movement of objects.

In the following chapters, the representation of a moving object, the management of moving objects and the data structure are given in section 2. And, in section 3, the BUMD-tree and the updating method of moving objects are described. The experimental results are shown in section 4. Finally, the summary is discussed in section 5.

2. Management of Moving Objects

In the applications of IoT, GIS, ITS, and monitoring systems, the background data such as roads, rivers and buildings do not change their locations or attributes in a short time. However, the moving objects may change their locations every unit time. It is necessary to manage two different type objects. These objects are represented as spatial data. A spatial data consists of geometrical patterns such as points, segments, rectangular and so forth in n-dimensional space. A location of an object is represented by $(x(t), y(t), t)$ in two-dimensional case where t is time, $(x(t), y(t))$ is a position of the object at t. Generally, the spatial data are managed by a hierarchical data structures such as kd, R, KDB, MD and other trees. Especially, the MD-tree is one of the most efficient data structures for managing the spatial data. In this section, the MD-tree is explained simply, because our proposed data structure is developed by extending the MD-tree. Then the update cost of data structure for moving objects is described.

2.1 The MD-tree

At first, a brief introduction of an MD-tree's data structure is described. Figure 1 illustrates the original MD-tree which is based on 2-3 tree. An MD-tree consists of two types of nodes; leaf and internal node. A node in the top of tree called a root. An internal node has pointers to children nodes. Objects are stored in only leaves. In the Figure 1, the capacity of a leaf is 3. Each node corresponds to a (hyper-) rectangular region. The root corresponds to the entire data space. A child node corresponds to a sub-region of the parent region. An MD-tree manages the locations of the objects, and the region corresponding to the root node of the MD-tree is divided into sub-regions according to the distribution of objects. If an object is inserted into a full leaf L, the corresponding region is split into two sub-regions such that at least half of objects in L are contained in each sub-region. Then a new leaf corresponding to one of the sub-regions is created, and objects in the sub-region are moved from L to the new leaf. An internal node and a leaf are defined as followings.

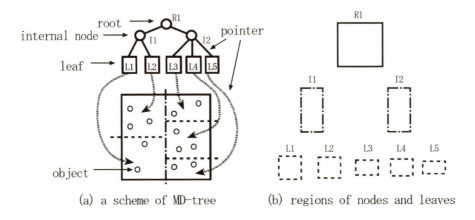

Figure 1. The original MD-tree

An internal node In has the following fields;

$$\text{Node In} = \{ \text{Rect\_m}, \text{P\_array}[3], \text{Rect\_c}\},$$

where Rect_m is a rectangle which encloses all rectangles of the lower nodes of In, P_array[3] is an array of child pointers, and Rect_c is a circumscribed rectangle which encloses all the data in the sub-tree rooted with In.

A leaf L has the following fields;

$$\text{Leaf L} = \{ \text{Rect\_m}, \text{D}[C], \text{Rect\_c}\},$$

where Rect_m is a rectangle corresponding to leaf L, D[C] is an array of pointers to the data, C is a capacity, and Rect_c is a circumscribed rectangle which encloses all the data in L.

In the search processing, the searching is executed from the root to leaves while checking the region of nodes and leaves. Then the object's data in leaves is retrieved. The MD-tree has properties that a tree structure is always balanced and the storage utilization rate is higher than 66.6%. The strict algorithms of the MD-tree are described in [5].

2.2 The Update Cost of Data Structure for Moving Objects

In the applications of IoT, GIS, ITS, monitoring and navigation systems for the moving objects such as squad cars, ambulances, fire engines, taxies, mobiles, or robots, the locations of moving objects must be immediately managed and monitored to conduct the movements or to make motion

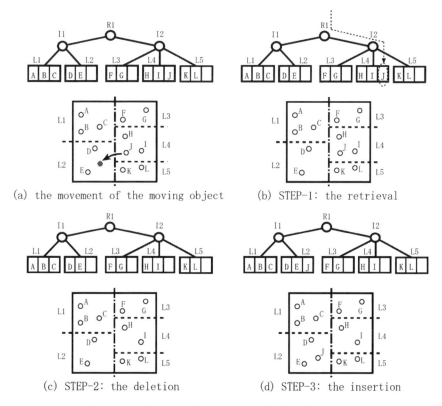

Figure 2. The example of a conventional update method

plans. In the data structure for managing moving objects, a moving object is a spatial data into which the location of itself changes as time passes. Therefore, the data structure such as kd, R, R*, KDB, MD and other trees must update situations of moving objects according to the progress of time since the newest version remains.

The conventional update method is shown in Figure 2. This method is executed in three steps in the data structure. At first, the moving object is retrieved based on its former location. Second, the found moving object is deleted. Finally, the moving object after it moves is inserted based on the current location. The advantages of this method is easy to perform the update of the data structure by the basic operation (retrieval, deletion, and insertion), and to manage both the moving objects and the static objects. However, the cost of this method increases in proportion to the number of updated objects, because there are three steps to update the location of an object. Moreover, when moving objects move every time, in other words, the locations of moving objects are constantly reported with the progress of time, the update cost becomes much higher. Therefore, it is very important to decrease the cost of update for the management of moving objects. The motivation of our research is to solve this problem; to cut-down the cost of update for moving objects. The BUMD-tree is proposed for managing moving objects.

3. The BUMD-tree

The novel concepts of the BUMD-tree are the butch insertion using a buffer array and the simplification of restructuring according to data insertion. In the conventional algorithm, when an object moves, it is necessary to find the object in the data structure (tree), delete it, and reinsert the object to store a new location. In addition, this process may cause an adjustment of the tree. The cost for updating the location of moving objects is proportional to the number of moving objects and the height of the tree. The cost is $O(N \times L)$, where N is the number of moving objects, and L is the height of the tree. In the BUMD-tree, to reduce the cost of the updating of the data structure, uses a buffer array in which reported new locations of the moving objects are stored.

3.1 Buffer Array

An example of batch manner is shown in Figure 3. At the first, locations of new moving objects are inserted in the buffer array (Figure 3 (a)). When the buffer array becomes full, the moving objects in the buffer array are inserted into the tree in a batch manner. From the root of a tree, a retrieval of the BUMD-tree visits sub-nodes recursively (Figure 3 (b)). When locations of moving objects are included in a region of a visited sub-node, the objects are moved to left side in the buffer array, and the other objects are moved to right side in the buffer array, as the BUMD-tree of quick sort do. When the retrieval reaches to a leaf, the location the moving objects in the buffer array are inserted into the leaf using the original insertion algorithm of the data structure (Figure 3 (c)). When the spatial data structure manages both moving objects and static objects together, new moving objects are inserted into places in leaves except the place where static objects and moving objects of same time are stored. Therefore, the stack objects remain in the data structure and it is possible to add the objects into the data structure without the deletion. In the Figure 3 (c), A, and C are moving objects, and B, D, and E are static objects. If a leaf is already full, the object that cannot be inserted is preserved in main memory by a link, an array, or other structures. Then, the other objects in the buffer array are inserted into a sub-tree (Figure 3 (d)). The BUMD-tree is presented in the followings. In this manner, when there are objects in the main memory, they are retrieved. Also, the search algorithm of the BUMD-tree is same as original MD-tree.

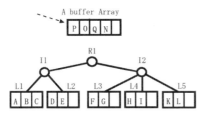
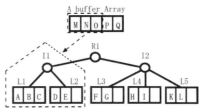
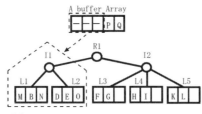
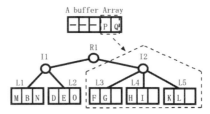

(a) Insertion new objects into a buffer array.

(b) Sort of a buffer array and insertion some objects into a sub-tree of I1.

(c) Insertion objects into leaves.

(d) Insertion other objects into a sub-tree of I2.

Figure 3. An example of batch manner

InsertBuffer(Ox, B, R)
Ox: Object
B: Buffer Array
R: Root
/* insert object Ox into B */
S1: Insert Ox into B, if B is not full. Return.
S2: Otherwise, Insert(B, R). Return.

Insert(B, N)
B: Buffer Array
N: An internal node
/* Insert objects in B into data structure */
S1: Set Nc to be a child node of N.
S2: (Bf, Bl) = Sort(B, Nc), where Bf and Bl is a part of B.
  S3: If Bf > 0, then
      If Nc is a leaf,
          If Nc is not full, Insert Bf into Nc. Else if Nc is full by static objects and new moving objects, then Bf holds on main memory. Otherwise, insert Bf into the place conserving old moving objects.
      Otherwise, Set Nc to be other child node of N, then Insert(Bf, Nc).
    Otherwise, set Nc to be other child node of N and Set B = Bl. Repeat from S2 to S3.
S4: Return.

Sort(B, Nc)
B: Buffer Array
Nc: An internal node
/* Sort of Buffer B */

S1: Let the first entry of B be Bf. Let the last entry of B be Bl.
S2: While(Bf is included in the region of Nc) Bf++.
S3: While(Bl is not included in the region of Nc) Bl--.
S4: Exchang Bf and Bl.
S5: Repeat from S2 to S4, if Bf > Bl. Otherwise, let objects which are included in the region of Cr are P. Return (Bf, Bl).

Moreover, in the BUMD-tree, the restructuring of the tree is not performed completely, because its cost is very high. Namely, the BUMD-tree uses the previous version of the data structure, and does not change the structural form of a tree. Moving objects are just inserted into the tree. The nodes and leaves of the tree are adjusted without deletions. Accordingly, the BUMD-tree does not update the data structure completely. The update cost can be reduced by this approach. However, it is expected that some search performances will decrease because the tree is not optimally adjusted.

3.2 Improvement of the BUMD-tree
In the BUMD-tree, there are large restrictions in this manner. These are presented as followings.

(1) It is not necessary to retrieve objects until all of them are updated at a time.
(2) There is no necessity for optimizing the data structure.
(3) The system can accept an increase of the capacity on the main memory when the location of moving objects is biased.

We improve the BUMD-tree to solve these problems by means of dual buffer arrays. The dual buffer array is illustrated in Figure 4 (a). The dual buffer array consists of the arrays for insertion and deletion. Static or moving objects which are inserted or new moving objects which moved, are stored in a buffer array for insertion. Also, static or moving objects which are deleted or old moving objects which moved at the past, are stored in a buffer array for deletion. The algorithm of sorting a dual array is the same as the BUMD-tree (Figure 4 (b)). In the leaf, objects in a buffer array for deletion are deleted, and then objects in a buffer array for insertion are inserted (Figure 4 (c) - (f)). Then, the data structure is updated according to the conditions of the original MD-tree; over-flow and under-flow[5] (Figure 4 (g)). The algorithm of the BUMD-tree is presented in the followings. In this manner, all objects in the dual array are inserted or deleted in the data structure when time changes, because the object in the main memory is not retrieved.

InsertAndDeleteBuffer(Ox1, Ox2, B1, B2, R)
Ox1: Object for insertion
Ox2: Object for deletion
B1: Buffer Array for insertion
B2: Buffer Array for deletion
R: Root
/* insert object Ox1 and Ox2 into B1 and B2 respectively*/
S1: Insert Ox1 into B1, if B1 is not full. And insert Ox2 into B2, if B2 is not full. Return.
S2: Otherwise, InsertAndDelete(B1, B2, R). Return.

InsertAndDelete(B1, B2, N)
B1: Buffer Array for insertion
B2: Buffer Array for deletion
N: An internal node
/* Insert objects in B1 and deletion objects in B2 */
S1: Set Nc to be a child node of N.
S2: (Bf1, Bl1) = Sort(B1, Nc), where Bf1 and Bl1 is a part of B1.
S3: (Bf2, Bl2) = Sort(B2, Nc), where Bf2 and Bl2 is a part of B2.
S4: If Bf1 > 0 or Bf2 > 0, then

If Nc is a leaf,
 If Bf2 > 0, delete Bf2 from Nc. And then, insert Bf2 into Nc , if Nc is not full.
 Otherwise, adjust data structure according to the conditions of the original MD-tree;
 over-flow and under-flow[5].
Otherwise, Set Nc to be other child node of N, then InsertAndDelete(Bf1, Bf2, Nc).

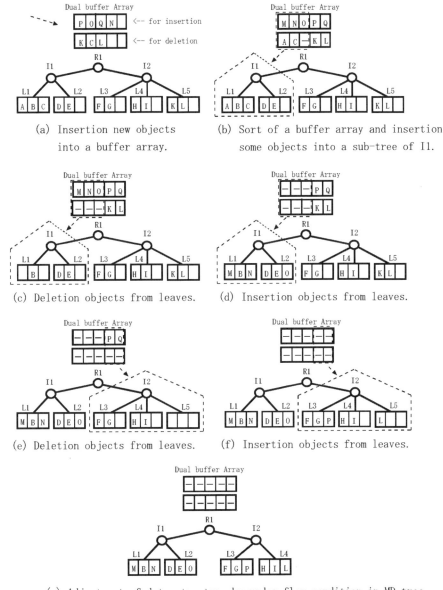

(a) Insertion new objects into a buffer array.
(b) Sort of a buffer array and insertion some objects into a sub-tree of I1.
(c) Deletion objects from leaves.
(d) Insertion objects from leaves.
(e) Deletion objects from leaves.
(f) Insertion objects from leaves.
(g) Adjustment of data structure by under-flow condition in MD-tree.

Figure 4. An example of the improved the BUMD-tree

Otherwise, set Nc to be other child node of N, set B1 = Bl1, and set B2 = Bl2. Repeat from S2 to S4.

S4: Return.

4. Experimental Results

To evaluate the performances and characteristics of the BUMD-tree and the conventional method, a series of simulation tests is carried out. The conventional method is executed in three steps; the retrieval, the deletion, and the insertion. The BUMD-tree with a buffer array called BUMDv1, and the BUMD-tree with dual buffer array called BUMDv2. The update requirement and the search performances are compared. The structural properties of the BUMDv1, the BUMDv2, and the conventional method are the same.

4.1 Experimental Conditions

The BUMDv1, the BUMDv2, and the conventional method manage the same data sets. The data set with 100,000 initial data is used. In the experiments, the number of moving objects is 10% of static objects (map components such as roads, buildings, etc) in data structure. Objects move with a rectilinear motion, and positions are sampled 100 times. Moving object is a point with the velocity (Vx, Vy). The speed of each object is given random within the maximum range [0, 10] per unit sampling time. The moving direction is also decided randomly. The buffer size of the BUMDv1 and the BUMDv2 are 2 x n, where n is from 7 to 11. The maximum number of child nodes is equal to 3, and the maximum number of objects in a leaf is 20. The entire data space is (10,000 x 10,000) square area. Objects' positions are generated randomly from a uniform distribution.

4.2 Experimental Results

Figure 5 shows the result of update cost which is evaluated by the total number of node and leaf accesses when 10,000 objects change their locations. This result is an average value for 100 experiments. Thus, the result is the number of visited nodes and leaves in processing of update at a time. As for the BUMDv1 and the BUMDv2, the update costs decrease according to enlarging of the size of the buffer. The reduction in the update cost can be achieved because the total number of visiting nodes and the number of the insertion processing can decrease by omitting deletion. The cost can be reduced to 1/B, where B is the number of moving object in a buffer array. As shown in the Figure 5, the update cost of the BUMDv1 and the BUMDv2 become less than the conventional method in any case. The number of visited nodes and leaves in the BUMDv1 is reduced to 74.8-91.3% of the conventional method. Also, the number of nodes and leaves in the BUMDv2 is 73.4-90.7% of the conventional method. Figure 6 shows the numbers of visited nodes and leaves in detail, when the size of the array is 1,024 in the Figure 5. In the BUMDv2, the update cost is improved (suppressed) about 5.6% compared with the BUMDv1. On the other hand, the number of objects in data structure is illustrated in Figure 7. In the BUMDv1, the number of objects inserted into a tree structure like MD-tree decreases by enlarging of the size of the buffer, because the moving objects, that cannot be inserted, are stored in main memory without adjustment of data structure. This means that the search performances will decrease. Finally, an experimental result for search performances is shown as Figure 8. The retrieval performances of the BUMDv1, the BUMDv2, and the conventional method almost become the same. However, this result is presented only the numbers of visited node and leaf. Therefore, the retrieval performance of the BUMDv1 is the worst, because the BUMDv1 should retrieve object on the main memory.

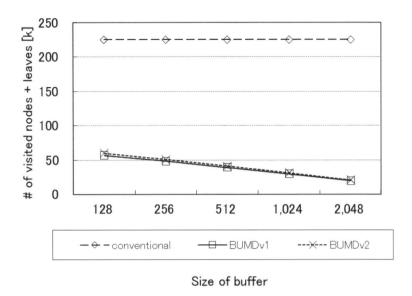

Figure 5. Update costs; Evaluated by visited nodes and leaves

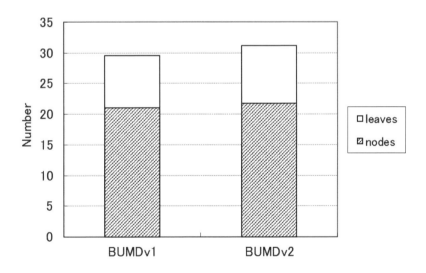

Figure 6. Detail update cost when the size of the array is 1,024
(# of visited nodes and leaves)

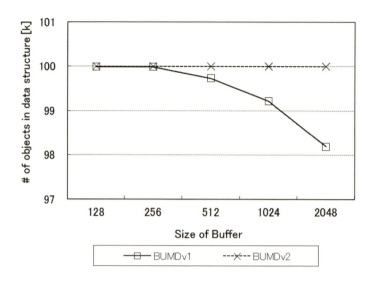

Figure 7. The number of objects inserted into a tree structure in the BUMDv1 and the BUMDv2

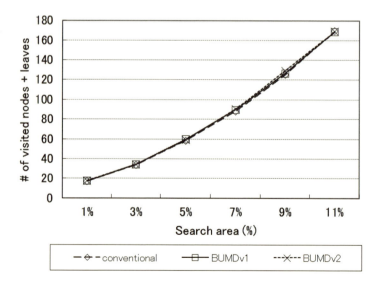

Figure 8. Result of search performances of the BUMDv1, the BUMDv2, and the conventional method

5. Conclusion

The new spatial data structure has been developed by extending the MD-tree for managing moving objects, such as IoT, GIS, ITS, monitoring systems and so on. The novel concepts of the BUMD-tree are a butch insertion using a buffer array or dual array, and a simplified restructuring according to the processes of data insertion and deletion. The search performances of the BUMD-tree were evaluated by simulation tests. In the BUMD-tree, the update cost decreases according to enlarging of the size of the buffer. The update cost in the BUMD-tree is about 73.4-91.3% of the conventional method. Also, the search efficiencies of the BUMD-tree and the conventional method are almost the same. The concept introduced in the BUMD-tree can be applied to hierarchical data structures such as kd, R, R*, KDB and other trees.

References

[1] J. L. Bentley, "K-d trees for Semidynamic Point Sets," Proc. ACM Symp. on 6th SCG, 1990, pp. 187-197.
[2] A. Guttman, "A Dynamic Index Structure for Spatial Searching," Proc. ACM SIGMOD, 1984, pp.47-57.
[3] N. Beckman, H. P. Kriegel, R. Schneider and B. Seeger, "R*-trees: An Efficient and Robust access Method for Points and Rectangles," Proc. ACM SIGMOD, 1990, pp.322-331.
[4] J. T. Robinson, "The KDB Tree: A Search Structure for Large Multidimensional Dynamic Indexes," Proc. ACM SIGMOD, 1981, pp. 10-18.
[5] Y. Nakamura, S. Abe, Y. Ohsawa and M. Sakauchi, "The MD-tree: An Efficient Data Management Strucuture for Spatial Objects," IEEE trans. KDE., Vol.5, No.4, 1993, pp.682-694.
[6] Y. Tao, J. Sun and D. Papadias, "Analysis of predictive spatio-temporal queries," ACM Trans. Database Syst., Vol.28, No.4, 2003, pp.295-336.
[7] S. Saltenis, C. S. Jensen and S. T. Leutenegger and M. A. Lopez, Indexing the Position of Continuously Moving Objects," Proc. ACM SIGMOD, 2000, pp331-342.
[8] Y. Tao, C. Faloutsos, D. Papadias and B. Liu, "Prediction and indexing of moving objects with unknown motion patterns," Proc. ACM SIGMOD, 2004, pp.611-622.
[9] D. Pfoser, C. S. Jensen and Y. Theodoridis, "Novel Approaches to the Indexing of Moving Object Trajectories," Proc. VLDB, 2000, pp10-14.
[10] J. Sun, D. Papadias, Y. Tao, and B. Liu, "Querying about the past, the present, the future in spatio-temporal databases," Proc. ICDE, 2004, pp.202-213.
[11] Y. Nakamura, H. Dekihara and R. Furukawa, "Spatio-Temporal Data Management for Moving Objects Using the PMD-Tree," Advances in Database Technology LNCS1552, Springer, 1999, pp.496-507.

Chapter 5

A Study on an Equivalent Penalty Coefficient Value for Adaptive Control of the Penalty Coefficient in Constrained Optimization by Differential Evolution

Setsuko Sakai* and Tetsuyuki Takahama**
*Faculty of Commercial Sciences, Hiroshima Shudo University
1-1 Ozuka-Higashi 1-chome, Asaminami-ku, Hiroshima, JAPAN 731-3195
**Graduate School of Information Sciences, Hiroshima City University
4-1 Ozuka-Higashi 3-chome, Asaminami-ku, Hiroshima, JAPAN 731-3194

Abstract

The penalty function method has been widely used for solving constrained optimization problems. In the method, an extended objective function, which is the sum of the objective value and the constraint violation weighted by the penalty coefficient, is optimized. However, it is difficult to control the coefficient properly because proper control varies in each problem. In this study, the equivalent penalty coefficient value (EPC) is proposed for population-based optimization algorithms (POAs). EPC can be defined in POAs where a new solution is compared with the old solution. EPC is the penalty coefficient value that makes the two extended objective values of the solutions the same. Search that gives priority to objective values is realized by selecting a small EPC in a population. Search that gives priority to constraint violations is realized by selecting a large EPC. It is expected that the adaptive control of the penalty coefficient can be realized by selecting an appropriate EPC. The proposed method is introduced to differential evolution. The nature of the proposed method is shown by solving several constrained optimization problems.

Key Words:
Constrained optimization, Nonlinear optimization, Equivalent penalty coefficient value, Population-based optimization, Differential evolution, Evolutionary algorithms

1. Introduction

Constrained optimization problems, especially nonlinear constrained optimization problems, where objective functions are minimized under given constraints, are very important and frequently appear in the real world. There exist many studies on solving constrained optimization problems using population-based optimization algorithms (POAs) such as evolutionary algorithms (EAs) [1–3] and particle swarm optimization (PSO) [4]. POAs basically lack a mechanism to incorporate the constraints of a given problem in the fitness value of individuals. Thus, many studies have been dedicated to handle the constraints in POAs.

The penalty function method has been widely used for solving constrained optimization problems. In the method, an extended objective function is optimized. The function is defined by the sum of the objective value and the constraint violation weighted by the penalty coefficient. Feasible solutions can be found by increasing the penalty coefficient into infinity theoretically. However, it is difficult to control the coefficient properly because proper control varies in each problem. In this study, an equivalent penalty coefficient value (EPC) is proposed for adaptive control of the penalty coefficient in POAs. EPC can be defined in POAs such as differential evolution (DE) and particle swarm optimization (PSO) where a new solution is compared with the old solution. For example, a child individual is compared with the parent individual in DE and a new position after moving is compared with the personal best position found so far in PSO. EPC is the penalty coefficient value that makes the two extended objective values of the old solution and the new solution the same when the objective values and the constraint violation are in a trade-off relationship. In POAs, there are plural EPCs in a population generally and the EPCs can be sorted in ascending order. Search that gives priority to objective values is realized by selecting a small EPC, or a high-order EPC. Search that gives priority to constraint violations is realized by selecting a large EPC, or a low-order EPC. It is expected that adaptive control of the penalty coefficient can be realized by selecting an appropriate EPC based on an order of EPCs. The proposed method is introduced to DE. The nature of the proposed method is shown by solving several well known constrained optimization problems.

In Section 2, constrained optimization problems are defined and constrained optimization methods are briefly reviewed. DE is explained in Section 3. The penalty function method and the proposed method are explained in Section 4. In Section 5, experimental results on three constrained problems are shown and the results of the proposed method are compared with those of other methods. Finally, conclusions are described in Section 6.

2. Solving Constrained Optimization Problems

2.1 Constrained Optimization Problems

The general constrained optimization problem (P) with inequality, equality, upper bound and lower bound constraints is defined as follows:

$$\begin{align}
\text{(P) minimize} \quad & f(\boldsymbol{x}), \tag{1}\\
\text{subject to} \quad & g_j(\boldsymbol{x}) \leq 0, \; j = 1, \ldots, q,\\
& h_j(\boldsymbol{x}) = 0, \; j = q+1, \ldots, m,\\
& l_i \leq x_i \leq u_i, \; i = 1, \ldots, D,
\end{align}$$

where $\boldsymbol{x} = (x_1, x_2, \cdots, x_D)$ is a D dimensional vector of decision variables, $f(\boldsymbol{x})$ is an objective function, $g_j(\boldsymbol{x}) \leq 0$ are q inequality constraints and $h_j(\boldsymbol{x}) = 0$ are $m - q$ equality constraints. The functions f, g_j and h_j are linear or nonlinear real-valued functions. The values u_i and l_i are the upper and lower bounds of x_i, respectively. All constraints define the *feasible region* $\mathcal{F}$. The upper and lower bound constraints define the *search space* $\mathcal{S}$. Feasible solutions exist in $\mathcal{F} \subseteq \mathcal{S}$.

2.2 Constrained Optimization Methods

POAs for constrained optimization can be classified into several categories according to the way the constraints are treated as follows [3]:

(1) Constraints are only used to see whether a search point is feasible or not. Approaches in this category are usually called death penalty methods. In this category, the searching process begins with one or more feasible points and continues to search for new points within the feasible region. When a new search point is generated and the point is not feasible, the point is repaired or discarded. When the feasible region is very small, generating initial feasible

points is difficult and computationally demanding. If the feasible region is extremely small, as in problems with equality constraints, it is almost impossible to find initial feasible points.

(2) The constraint violation, which is the sum of the violation of all constraint functions, is combined with the objective function. The penalty function method is in this category [5–8]. In the penalty function method, an extended objective function is defined by adding the constraint violation to the objective function as a penalty. The optimization of the objective function and the constraint violation is realized by the optimization of the extended objective function. The main difficulty of the penalty function method is the selection of an appropriate value for the penalty coefficient that adjusts the strength of the penalty. If the penalty coefficient is large, feasible solutions can be obtained, but the optimization of the objective function will be insufficient. On the contrary, if the penalty coefficient is small, high quality (but infeasible) solutions can be obtained as it is difficult to decrease the constraint violation. In order to solve the difficulty, some methods, where the penalty coefficient is adaptively controlled, are proposed [9, 10].

(3) The constraint violation and the objective function are used separately. In this category, both the constraint violation and the objective function are optimized by a lexicographic order in which the constraint violation precedes the objective function. Deb [11] proposed a method that adopts the extended objective function, which realizes the lexicographic ordering. Takahama and Sakai proposed the α constrained method [12] and ε constrained method [13] that adopt a lexicographic ordering with relaxation of the constraints. Runarsson and Yao [14] proposed the stochastic ranking method that adopts the stochastic lexicographic order, which ignores the constraint violation with some probability. Mezura-Montes and Coello [15] proposed a comparison mechanism that is equivalent to the lexicographic ordering. Venkatraman and Yen [16] proposed a two-step optimization method, which first optimizes the constraint violation and then the objective function. These methods were successfully applied to various problems.

(4) The constraints and the objective function are optimized by multiobjective optimization methods. In this category, the constrained optimization problems are solved as the multiobjective optimization problems in which the objective function and the constraint functions are objectives to be optimized [17–23]. But in many cases, solving multiobjective optimization problems is a more difficult and expensive task than solving single objective optimization problems.

(5) Hybridization methods. In this category, constrained problems are solved by combining some of the above mentioned methods. Mallipeddi and Suganthan [24] proposed a hybridization of the methods in the categories (2), (3) and (4).

In this study, the category (2) is paid attention to. A simple and effective control of the penalty coefficient using EPC is proposed.

3. Differential Evolution

DE is an evolutionary algorithm proposed by Storn and Price [25, 26]. DE has been successfully applied to the optimization problems including non-linear, non-differentiable, non-convex and multimodal functions. It has been shown that DE is fast and robust to these functions [27].

In DE, initial individuals are randomly generated within given search space and form an initial population. Each individual $x_i, i = 1, 2, \cdots, N$ contains D genes as decision variables, where N

is the population size. At each generation or iteration, all individuals are selected as parents. Each parent is processed as follows: The mutation operation begins by choosing several individuals from the population except for the parent in the processing. The first individual is a base vector. All subsequent individuals are paired to create difference vectors. The difference vectors are scaled by a scaling factor F and added to the base vector. The resulting vector, or a mutant vector, is then recombined with the parent. The probability of recombination at an element is controlled by a crossover rate CR. This crossover operation produces a child, or a trial vector. Finally, for survivor selection, the trial vector is accepted for the next generation if the child is better than the parent.

There are some variants of DE that have been proposed. The variants are classified using the notation DE/*base*/*num*/*cross* such as DE/rand/1/bin and DE/rand/1/exp.

"*base*" specifies a way of selecting an individual that will form the base vector. For example, DE/rand selects an individual for the base vector at random from the population. DE/best selects the best individual in the population.

"*num*" specifies the number of difference vectors used to perturb the base vector. In case of DE/rand/1, for example, for each parent x_i, three individuals x_{p1}, x_{p2} and x_{p3} are chosen randomly from the population without overlapping x_i and each other. A new vector, or a mutant vector m_i is generated by the base vector x_{p1} and the difference vector $x_{p2} - x_{p3}$, where F is the scaling factor.

$$m_i = x_{p1} + F(x_{p2} - x_{p3}) \qquad (2)$$

"*cross*" specifies the type of crossover that is used to create a child. For example, 'bin' indicates that the binomial crossover in which the elements of the mutant vector are inherited to the child with a constant crossover rate is used. 'exp' indicates that the exponential crossover in which the elements of the mutant vector is inherited with exponentially decreasing the crossover rate is used. The exponential crossover is a kind of two-point crossover. Figure 1 shows the binomial and exponential crossover. A new child x'_i is generated from the parent x_i and the mutant vector m_i, where CR is a crossover rate.

```
binomial crossover DE/·/·/bin
    j_rand=randint(1,D);
    for(k=1; k≤D; k++) {
        if(k == j_rand  ||  u(0,1) < CR)   x'_{ik}=m_{ik};
        else  x'_{ik}=x_{ik};
    }
exponential crossover DE/·/·/exp
    k=1; j=randint(1,D);
    do {
        x'_{ij}=m_{ij};
        k=k+1; j=(j+1)%D;
    } while(k≤D && u(0,1) < CR);
    while(k≤D) {
        x'_{ij}=x_{ij};
        k=k+1; j=(j+1)%D;
    }
```

Figure 1. Binomial and exponential crossover, where $randint(1, D)$ generates an integer randomly from $[1, D]$ and $u(l, r)$ is a uniform random number generator in $[l, r]$.

The algorithm of DE is as follows:

Step1 Initialization of a population.

Initial N individuals $P = \{\boldsymbol{x}_i, i = 1, 2, \cdots, N\}$ are generated randomly in search space and form an initial population.

Step2 Termination condition.

If the number of function evaluations exceeds the maximum number of function evaluations $FE_{\max}$, the algorithm is terminated.

Step3 DE operations.

Each individual $\boldsymbol{x}_i$ is selected as a parent. A mutant vector $\boldsymbol{m}_i$ is generated according to Eq. (2). A trial vector (child) is generated from the parent $\boldsymbol{x}_i$ and the mutant vector $\boldsymbol{m}_i$ using a crossover operation shown in Figure 1. If the child is better than the parent, or the DE operation is succeeded, the child survives. Otherwise the parent survives. Go back to Step3 and the next individual is selected as a parent until all individuals are processed.

Step4 Survivor selection (generation change).

The population is organized by the survivors. Go back to Step2.

Figure 2 shows a pseudo-code of DE/rand/1.

```
DE/rand/1()
{
// Initialize an population
 P=N individuals generated randomly in the search space S;
 FE=N;
 for(t=1; FE ≤ FE_max; t++) {
   for(i=1; i ≤ N; i++) {
// DE operation
     x_p1=Randomly selected from P(p1 ≠ i);
     x_p2=Randomly selected from P(p2 ∉ {i,p1});
     x_p3=Randomly selected from P(p3 ∉ {i,p1,p2});
     m_i=x_p1+F(x_p2 − x_p3);
     x'_i=trial vector is generated from x_i and m_i
           by the crossover operation;
// Survivor selection
     if(f(x'_i) < f(x_i))  z_i=x'_i;
     else                  z_i=x_i;
     FE=FE+1;
   }
   P={z_i,  i = 1, 2, ··· , N};
 }
}
```

Figure 2. A pseudo-code of DE, where FE is the number of function evaluations.

4. Proposed Method

4.1 The Penalty Function Method

In the constrained optimization, it is necessary to optimize the objective function and the constraint violation simultaneously. In the penalty function method, the constrained optimization problem is converted to the following unconstrained optimization problem by adding the constraint violation $\phi(\boldsymbol{x})$ weighted by the penalty coefficient to the objective function $f(\boldsymbol{x})$ as a penalty.

$$F(\boldsymbol{x}) = f(\boldsymbol{x}) + \rho\phi(\boldsymbol{x}) \tag{3}$$

where $F(\cdot)$ is the extended objective function and ρ is the penalty coefficient ($\rho > 0$). By increasing the penalty coefficient towards ∞, the constraint violation converges to 0, and an feasible solution can be obtained.

The constraint violation $\phi(\boldsymbol{x})$ satisfies the following:

$$\begin{cases} \phi(\boldsymbol{x}) = 0 \ (\boldsymbol{x} \in \mathcal{F}) \\ \phi(\boldsymbol{x}) > 0 \ (\boldsymbol{x} \notin \mathcal{F}) \end{cases} \tag{4}$$

Some types of constraint violations, which are adopted as a penalty in penalty function methods, can be defined as follows:

$$\phi(\boldsymbol{x}) = \max\{\max_j\{0, g_j(\boldsymbol{x})\}, \max_j |h_j(\boldsymbol{x})|\} \tag{5}$$

$$\phi(\boldsymbol{x}) = \sum_j max\{0, g_j(\boldsymbol{x})\}^p + \sum_j |h_j(\boldsymbol{x})|^p \tag{6}$$

where p is a positive number.

4.2 Equivalent Penalty Coefficient Value

Let assume the POAs where a new solution $\boldsymbol{x}'_i$ is compared with the old solution $\boldsymbol{x}_i$ and the old solution is replaced with the new solution only if the new solution is better than the old solution. When both of the objective value and the constraint violation of $\boldsymbol{x}'_i$ are better than those of $\boldsymbol{x}_i$, the value of the extended objective function of $\boldsymbol{x}'_i$ is always better than that of $\boldsymbol{x}_i$, or $F(\boldsymbol{x}') < F(\boldsymbol{x})$ for any ρ, and vice versa. Also, if the objective values and the constraint violations are the same, $F(\boldsymbol{x}) = F(\boldsymbol{x}')$ holds for any ρ. Therefore, if the following conditions are satisfied, there is no need to determine the penalty coefficient.

$$f(\boldsymbol{x}') \leq f(\boldsymbol{x}) \text{ and } \phi(\boldsymbol{x}') \leq \phi(\boldsymbol{x}) \text{ or } f(\boldsymbol{x}) \leq f(\boldsymbol{x}') \text{ and } \phi(\boldsymbol{x}) \leq \phi(\boldsymbol{x}') \tag{7}$$

Otherwise, there exist a solution with a better objective value and a worse violation value and a solution with a worse objective value and a better violation value. The equivalent penalty coefficient value (EPC) ρ_i is defined as the value that makes the extended objective values of $\boldsymbol{x}_i$ and $\boldsymbol{x}'_i$ the same:

$$F(\boldsymbol{x}_i) = F(\boldsymbol{x}'_i) \tag{8}$$

$$f(\boldsymbol{x}_i) + \rho_i\phi(\boldsymbol{x}_i) = f(\boldsymbol{x}'_i) + \rho_i\phi(\boldsymbol{x}'_i) \tag{9}$$

$$\rho_i = -\frac{f(\boldsymbol{x}_i) - f(\boldsymbol{x}'_i)}{\phi(\boldsymbol{x}_i) - \phi(\boldsymbol{x}'_i)} \tag{10}$$

Let assume that $f(\boldsymbol{x}_i) < f(\boldsymbol{x}'_i)$ and $\phi(\boldsymbol{x}'_i) < \phi(\boldsymbol{x}_i)$. If the penalty coefficient is larger than ρ_i, $F(\boldsymbol{x}'_i) < F(\boldsymbol{x}_i)$ is satisfied and $\boldsymbol{x}'_i$ is the better solution. On the contrary, if the penalty coefficient is smaller than ρ_i, $F(\boldsymbol{x}_i) < F(\boldsymbol{x}'_i)$ is satisfied and $\boldsymbol{x}_i$ is the better solution.

Let consider the list of ρ_i sorted in ascending order, $H = \{\rho_k \,|\, \rho_k < \rho_{k+1}, k = 1, 2, \cdots\}$ ($|H| \leq N$). In order to control the penalty coefficient simply and adaptively, an algorithm parameter R_{cp} (≥ 0), which is a constraint priority rate, is introduced. The coefficient ρ is decided as the $R_{cp}|H|$-th element in H using linear interpolation as follows:

$$\rho = \begin{cases} R_{cp}\rho_{|H|} & (R_{cp} > 1) \\ R_{cp}|H|\rho_1 & (\lfloor R_{cp}|H|\rfloor < 1) \\ \rho_{\lfloor R_{cp}|H|\rfloor} + (R_{cp}|H| - \lfloor R_{cp}|H|\rfloor)(\rho_{\lceil R_{cp}|H|\rceil} - \rho_{\lfloor R_{cp}|H|\rfloor}) & \text{(otherwise)} \end{cases} \quad (11)$$

where $|H|$ is the number of elements in H, $\lfloor \cdot \rfloor$ is rounding down to the nearest integer and $\lceil \cdot \rceil$ is rounding up to the nearest integer. The second equation is the interpolation between 0 and ρ_1. When $R_{cp} = 0$, only the objective value will be optimized because $\rho = 0$. When $R_{cp} > 1$, only the constraint violation will be optimized because $\rho > \rho_{|H|}$ and the constraint violation has always higher priority than the objective value. Setting $R_{cp} > 1$ has similar effect of $\rho = \infty$ in the ordinary penalty function method. It is thought that a feasible solution can be found by changing R_{cp} to over 1 theoretically. In this study, numerical experiments are performed as R_{cp} is fixed.

4.3 The Algorithm of the Proposed Method

The algorithm of the proposed method DEEPC (DE with EPC) is as follows:

Step1 Initialization of a population.

Initial N individuals $P = \{\boldsymbol{x}_i, i = 1, 2, \cdots, N\}$ are generated randomly in the search space and form an initial population. All individuals are evaluated.

Step2 Termination condition.

If the number of function evaluations exceeds the maximum number of function evaluations $FE_{\max}$, the algorithm is terminated.

Step3 DE operations.

The following operations are applied to all individuals $\boldsymbol{x}_i$ in the order of $i = 1, 2, \cdots, N$. A mutant vector $\boldsymbol{m}_i$ is generated according to Eq. (2). A trial vector (child) is generated from the parent $\boldsymbol{x}_i$ and the mutant vector $\boldsymbol{m}_i$ using a crossover operation shown in Figure 1. The child is evaluated.

Step4 Decision of the penalty coefficient value.

EPCs (ρ_i) are obtained as follows: If the individual i does not satisfy Eq.(7), ρ_i is calculated according to Eq.(10). H is obtained by sorting the list $\{\rho_i\}$ in ascending order. The penalty coefficient value ρ is decided according to Eq.(11).

Step5 Survivor selection (generation change).

Each child is compared with the parent in the order of $i = 1, 2, \cdots, N$ as follows: The extended objective values of the parent and the child are obtained. If the extended objective value of the child is better than that of the parent, the child survives. Otherwise the parent survives. If all survivors are determined, the population is replaced with the survivors. Go back to Step2.

5. Solving Nonlinear Optimization Problems

5.1 Test Problems and Experimental Conditions

In this study, three constrained optimization problems are tested: Himmelblau's problem, welded beam design problem and pressure vessel design problem, which are solved by various methods and compared in [2]. In the following, other results than the proposed method DEEPC are taken from [2].

The constraint violation is defined by Eq.(6) with p=1. The parameters for DE are: The number of individuals N=20, F=0.8, CR=0.95 and the exponential crossover is adopted. As for DEEPC, DEEPCs with R_{cp}=0.5, 0.6, 0.7, 0.8, 0.9, 1.0 and 1.1 are examined. The maximum number of function evaluations $FE_{\max}$=2,500, 5,000 and 10,000. For each problem, 30 independent runs are performed.

5.2 Himmelblau's Nonlinear Optimization Problem

Himmelblau's problem was originally given by Himmelblau [28], and it has been used as a benchmark for several GA-based methods that use penalties. In this problem, there are 5 decision variables, 6 nonlinear inequality constraints and 10 boundary conditions.

This problem can be defined as follows:

$$\text{Minimize } f(\boldsymbol{x}) = 5.3578547 x_3^2 + 0.8356891 x_1 x_5 + 37.293239 x_1 - 40792.141$$
$$\text{Subject to } g_1(\boldsymbol{x}) = 85.334407 + 0.0056858 x_2 x_5 + 0.00026 x_1 x_4 - 0.0022053 x_3 x_5,$$
$$g_2(\boldsymbol{x}) = 80.51249 + 0.0071317 x_2 x_5 + 0.0029955 x_1 x_2 + 0.0021813 x_3^2,$$
$$g_3(\boldsymbol{x}) = 9.300961 + 0.0047026 x_3 x_5 + 0.0012547 x_1 x_3 + 0.0019085 x_3 x_4,$$
$$0 \leq g_1(\boldsymbol{x}) \leq 92, 90 \leq g_2(\boldsymbol{x}) \leq 110, 20 \leq g_3(\boldsymbol{x}) \leq 25,$$
$$78 \leq x_1 \leq 102, 33 \leq x_2 \leq 45, 27 \leq x_3, x_4, x_5 \leq 45.$$

This problem was originally solved using the Generalized Reduced Gradient method (GRG) [28]. Gen and Cheng [29] used a genetic algorithm based on both local and global reference. The problem was solved using death penalty [2] in the first category and various penalty function approaches in the second category such as static penalty [5], dynamic penalty [6], annealing penalty [7], adaptive penalty [30] and Co-evolutionary penalty [8]. Also, the problem was solved using MGA (multiobjective genetic algorithm) [19] in the fourth category.

Experimental results on the problem are shown in Table 1 which include the results of DEEPC with changing R_{cp}. In each run, the best individual, which has the minimum constraint violation or has the best objective value if the violation is same, is recorded. The columns labeled Best, Average, Worst and S.D. are the best objective value, the average objective value, the worst objective value and the standard deviation of the objective values for the best individuals in 30 runs, respectively. The best results are highlighted by bold fonts.

The good methods were DEEPC, Co-evolutionary penalty method and MGA. Note that MGA and other penalty based approaches performed 5,000 function evaluations (FEs) while Co-evolutionary penalty method performed 900,000 FEs.

As for DEEPC, DEEPC with R_{cp}=0.6 attained the best average result of -31024.3907 in 2,500 FEs, the best average result of -31025.5570 in 5,000 FEs, and the best average result of -31025.5602 in 10,000 FEs. It is thought that DEEPC with R_{cp}=0.6 is the best method in all settings of R_{cp}. Also, DEEPC with R_{cp}=0.6, 0.7, 0.8, 0.9, 1.0 and 1.1 attained the best average result of -31025.5602 in 10,000 FEs. Only in 2,500 FEs, DEEPC with R_{cp}=0.6, 0.7, 0.8, 0.9, 1.0 and 1.1 can find better solutions on average than those of all other methods. Almost all DEEPCs except for R_{cp}=0.5 can find better solutions less than 1/2 FEs compared with other methods. So, DEEPC is the best method which can find very good solutions most efficiently and most stably.

Figure 3 shows the graphs of the average values over 30 runs for the objective value of the best individual and ρ over the number of FEs obtained by DEEPC with R_{cp}=0.5, 0.6, 0.7, 0.8, 0.9, 1.0

Table 1. Results of Himmelblau's problem

Algorithm	FEs	Best	Average	Worst	S.D.
DEEPC	2,500	-31023.8438	-30976.7515	-30803.7989	53.2969
(R_{cp}=0.5)	5,000	-31024.2758	-30976.7674	-30803.7989	53.3111
	10,000	-31024.2758	-30976.7674	-30803.7989	53.3111
DEEPC	2,500	-31025.3068	**-31024.3907**	**-31021.4895**	**0.8698**
(R_{cp}=0.6)	5,000	**-31025.5601**	**-31025.5570**	**-31025.5501**	**0.0028**
	10,000	**-31025.5602**	**-31025.5602**	**-31025.5602**	**0.0000**
DEEPC	2,500	**-31025.3372**	-31023.7448	-31019.3236	1.7225
(R_{cp}=0.7)	5,000	-31025.5600	-31025.5545	-31025.5020	0.0106
	10,000	**-31025.5602**	**-31025.5602**	**-31025.5602**	**0.0000**
DEEPC	2,500	-31025.1991	-31023.0910	-31015.1764	2.0184
(R_{cp}=0.8)	5,000	-31025.5594	-31025.5474	-31025.5238	0.0109
	10000	**-31025.5602**	**-31025.5602**	**-31025.5602**	**0.0000**
DEEPC	2,500	-31025.0413	-31022.7568	-31015.2690	2.7030
(R_{cp}=0.9)	5,000	-31025.5596	-31025.5453	-31025.4172	0.0257
	10,000	**-31025.5602**	**-31025.5602**	**-31025.5602**	**0.0000**
DEEPC	2,500	-31025.1908	-31020.2448	-30988.6398	7.0169
(R_{cp}=1.0)	5,000	-31025.5591	-31025.5240	-31025.1781	0.0716
	10,000	**-31025.5602**	**-31025.5602**	**-31025.5602**	**0.0000**
DEEPC	2,500	-31025.1908	-31022.3305	-31011.0797	2.8267
(R_{cp}=1.1)	5,000	-31025.5591	-31025.5393	-31025.3635	0.0383
	10,000	**-31025.5602**	**-31025.5602**	**-31025.5602**	**0.0000**
MGA	5,000	-31005.7966	-30862.8735	-30721.0418	73.240
Gen		-30183.576	N/A	N/A	N/A
GRG		-30373.949	N/A	N/A	N/A
Co-evolutionary	900,000	-31020.859	-30984.2407	-30792.4077	73.6335
Static	5,000	-30790.2716	-30446.4618	-29834.3847	226.3428
Dynamic	5,000	-30903.877	-30539.9156	-30106.2498	200.035
Annealing	5,000	-30829.201	-30442.126	-29773.085	244.619
Adaptive	5,000	-30903.877	-30448.007	-29926.1544	249.485
Death	5,000	-30790.271	-30429.371	-29834.385	234.555

and 1.1. Figure 4 shows the graphs of the average values over 30 runs for the average constraint violation in the population and the feasible rate which is the rate of the feasible solutions in the population.

As for the objective value, the value was converged to almost the same value except for DEEPC with R_{cp}=0.5. As for the value of ρ, the value was increasing rapidly in an early stage and was gradually decreasing after reaching a maximum value in general. However, in DEEPC with R_{cp}=0.9, 1.0 and 1.1, ρ was changed to a very large value and returned to a smaller value repeatedly. Larger R_{cp} tends to result in larger ρ.

As for the average violation, DEEPC with R_{cp}=0.5 failed to reduce the violation, DEEPC with R_{cp}=0.6, 0.7, 0.8 and 0.9 reduced the violation gradually, and DEEPC with R_{cp}=1.0 and 1.1 reduced the violation rapidly. As for the feasible rate, DEEPC with R_{cp}=0.5 reduced the feasible rate to 0 and failed to optimize the violation. DEEPC with R_{cp}=0.6 reduced the feasible rate to 0.3 but obtained the feasible solution with good objective values as mentioned before. DEEPC with

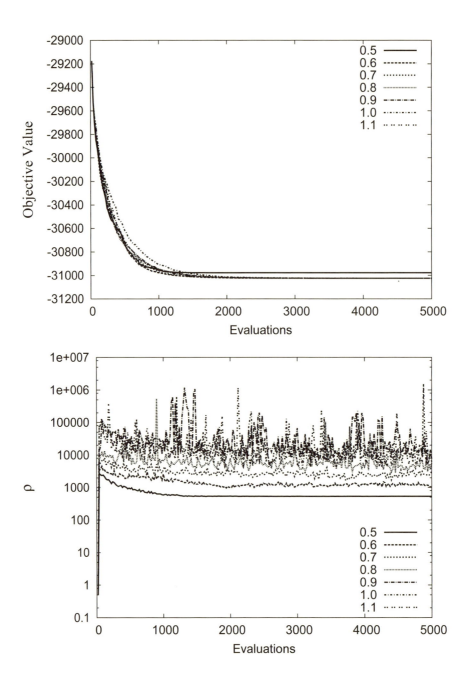

Figure 3. The graphs of the average values for the objective value and the penalty coefficient over the number of function evaluations in Himmelblau's problem.

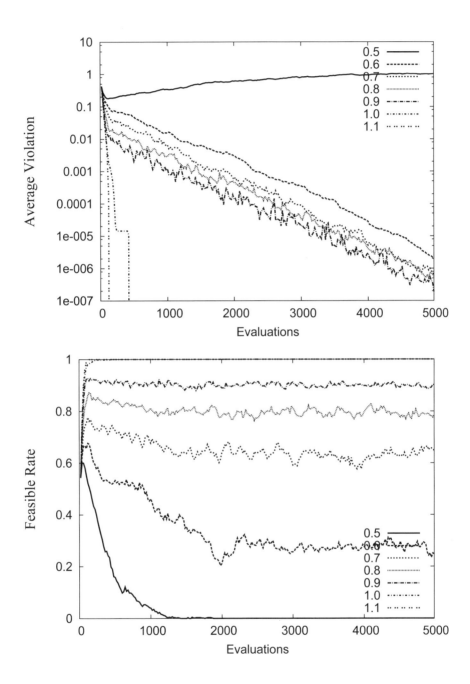

Figure 4. The graphs of the average values for the average constraint violation and the feasible rate over the number of function evaluations in Himmelblau's problem.

R_{cp}=0.7, 0.8 and 0.9 attained the feasible rate of about 0.7, 0.8 and 0.9, respectively. DEEPC with R_{cp}=1.0 and 1.1 attained the feasible rate of 1.0.

Therefore, it is thought that DEEPC with R_{cp}=0.6, 0.7 and 0.8 attained proper control of ρ and kept a proper feasible rate with balancing the optimization of the objective value and the constraint violation.

5.3 Welded Beam Design

The structure of a welded beam is shown in Figure 5. A welded beam is designed for minimum cost subject to constraints on shear stress (τ), bending stress in the beam (σ), buckling load on the bar (P_c), end deflection of the beam (δ) and side constraints [31]. There are 4 design variables: weld thickness $h(x_1)$, length of weld $l(x_2)$, width of the beam $t(x_3)$, thickness of the beam $b(x_4)$ in Figure 5. The problem has 7 inequality constraints.

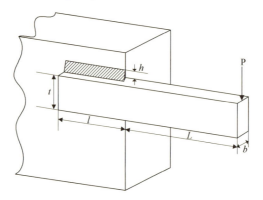

Figure 5. Welded beam design

This problem can be defined as follows:

$$\text{Minimize } f(\boldsymbol{x}) = 1.10471 x_1^2 x_2 + 0.04811 x_3 x_4 (14 + x_2)$$

Subject to $g_1(\boldsymbol{x}) = \tau(\boldsymbol{x}) - \tau_{max} \leq 0, g_2(\boldsymbol{x}) = \sigma(\boldsymbol{x}) - \sigma_{max} \leq 0,$

$g_3(\boldsymbol{x}) = x_1 - x_4 \leq 0,$

$g_4(\boldsymbol{x}) = 0.10471 x_1^2 + 0.04811 x_3 x_4 (14 + x_2) - 5 \leq 0,$

$g_5(\boldsymbol{x}) = 0.125 - x_1 \leq 0, g_6(\boldsymbol{x}) = \delta(\boldsymbol{x}) - \delta_{max} \leq 0,$

$g_7(\boldsymbol{x}) = P - P_c(\boldsymbol{x}) \leq 0, 0.1 \leq x_1, x_4 \leq 2, 0.1 \leq x_2, x_3 \leq 10,$

where

$$\tau = \sqrt{\tau'^2 + 2\tau'\tau'' \frac{x_2}{2R} + \tau''^2}, \tau' = \frac{P}{\sqrt{2} x_1 x_2}, \tau'' = \frac{MR}{J},$$

$$M = P\left(L + \frac{x_2}{2}\right), R = \sqrt{\frac{x_2^2 + (x_1 + x_3)^2}{4}},$$

$$J = 2\sqrt{2} x_1 x_2 \left(\frac{x_2^2}{12} + \frac{(x_1 + x_3)^2}{4}\right), \sigma(\boldsymbol{x}) = \frac{6PL}{x_4 x_3^2},$$

$$\delta(\boldsymbol{x}) = \frac{4PL^3}{E x_3^3 x_4}, Pc(\boldsymbol{x}) = \frac{4.013 E \sqrt{x_3^2 x_4^6 / 36}}{L^2} \left(1 - \frac{x_3}{2L}\sqrt{\frac{E}{4G}}\right),$$

$P = 6000 lb, L = 14 in, \delta_{max} = 0.25 in, E = 30 \times 10^6 psi,$

$G = 12 \times 10^6 psi, \tau_{max} = 13600 psi, \sigma_{max} = 30000 psi.$

Experimental results on the problem are shown in Table 2. The good methods were DEEPC and Co-evolutionary penalty method. Note that Co-evolutionary penalty method performed 900,000 FEs.

Table 2. Results of welded beam design

Algorithm	FEs	Best	Average	Worst	S.D.
DEEPC	2,500	1.8008	2.0310	2.8084	0.2357
(R_{cp}=0.5)	5,000	1.8008	2.0310	2.8084	0.2357
	10,000	1.8008	2.0310	2.8084	0.2357
DEEPC	2,500	1.7673	1.8676	2.0204	0.0640
(R_{cp}=0.6)	5,000	1.7673	1.8676	2.0204	0.0640
	10,000	1.7673	1.8676	2.0204	0.0640
DEEPC	2,500	1.7328	1.7880	1.8856	0.0412
(R_{cp}=0.7)	5,000	1.7250	1.7871	1.8856	0.0423
	10,000	**1.7249**	1.7871	1.8856	0.0423
DEEPC	2,500	1.7275	1.7342	1.7556	0.0059
(R_{cp}=0.8)	5,000	**1.7249**	1.7250	1.7256	0.0001
	10,000	**1.7249**	**1.7249**	**1.7249**	**0.0000**
DEEPC	2,500	**1.7259**	1.7324	**1.7393**	**0.0036**
(R_{cp}=0.9)	5,000	**1.7249**	**1.7249**	1.7251	0.0001
	10,000	**1.7249**	**1.7249**	**1.7249**	**0.0000**
DEEPC	2,500	1.7272	**1.7318**	1.7432	0.0037
(R_{cp}=1.0)	5,000	**1.7249**	**1.7249**	**1.7250**	**0.0000**
	10,000	**1.7249**	**1.7249**	**1.7249**	**0.0000**
DEEPC	2,500	1.7263	1.7326	1.7488	0.0054
(R_{cp}=1.1)	5,000	**1.7249**	**1.7249**	1.7251	**0.0000**
	10,000	**1.7249**	**1.7249**	**1.7249**	**0.0000**
MGA	5,000	1.8245	1.9190	1.9950	0.05377
Co-evolutionary	900,000	1.7483	1.7720	1.7858	0.01122
Static	5,000	2.0469	2.9728	4.5741	0.6196
Dynamic	5,000	2.1062	3.1556	5.0359	0.7006
Annealing	5,000	2.0713	2.9533	4.1261	0.4902
Adaptive	5,000	1.9589	2.9898	4.84036	0.6515
Death	5,000	2.0821	3.1158	4.5138	0.6625

As for DEEPC, DEEPC with R_{cp}=1.0 attained the best average result of 1.7318 in 2,500 FEs, the best average result of 1.7249 in 5,000 FEs and also in 10,000 FEs. It is thought that DEEPC with R_{cp}=1.0 is the best method in all settings of R_{cp}. Also, DEEPC with R_{cp}=0.8, 0.9, 1.0 and 1.1 attained the best average result of 1.7249 in 10,000 FEs. Only in 2,500 FEs, DEEPC with R_{cp}=0.8, 0.9, 1.0 and 1.1 can find better solutions on average than those of all other methods. DEEPCs except for R_{cp}=0.5, 0.6 and 0.7 can find better solutions less than 1/2 FEs compared with other methods. So, DEEPC is the best method which can find very good solutions most efficiently and most stably.

Figure 6 shows the graphs of the average values over 30 runs for the objective value of the best individual and ρ over the number of FEs obtained by DEEPC. Figure 7 shows the graphs of the average values over 30 runs for the average constraint violation in the population and the feasible rate.

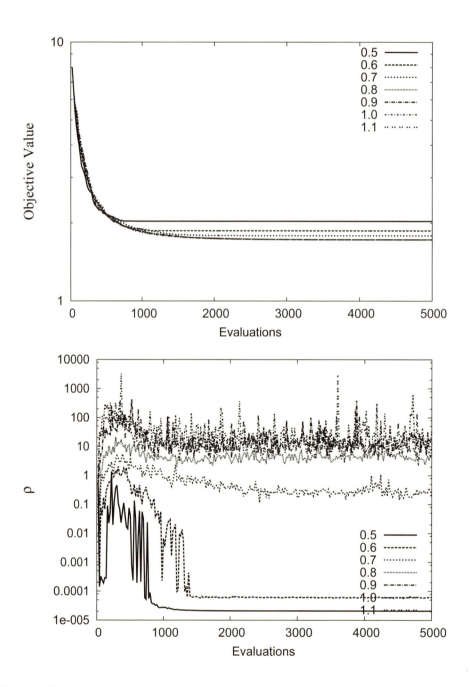

Figure 6. The graphs of the average values for the objective value and the penalty coefficient over the number of function evaluations in welded beam design problem.

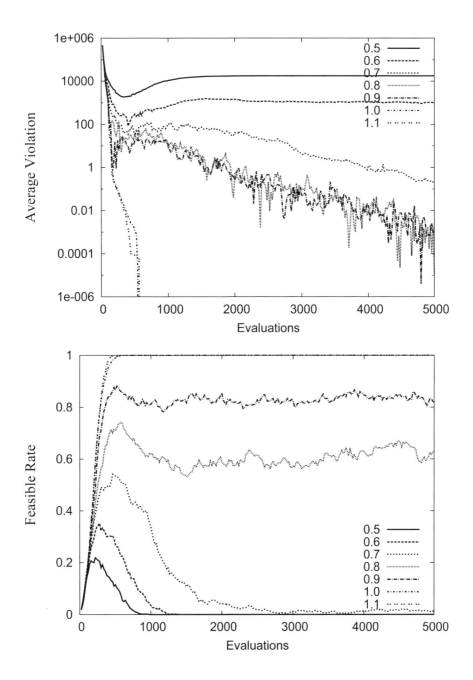

Figure 7. The graphs of the average values for the average constraint violation and the feasible rate over the number of function evaluations in welded beam design problem.

As for the objective value, the value was converged to almost the same value except for DEEPC with R_{cp}=0.5, 0.6 and 0.7. As for the value of ρ, the value was increasing rapidly in an early stage and was decreasing gradually and smoothly in DEEPC with R_{cp}=0.7, 0.8 and 0.9, and was decreasing with large vibration in other settings of DEEPC. Larger R_{cp} tends to result in larger ρ.

As for the average violation, DEEPC with R_{cp}=0.5 and 0.6 failed to reduce the violation, DEEPC with R_{cp}=0.7 reduced the violation very slowly, DEEPC with R_{cp}=0.8 and 0.9 reduced the violation gradually, and DEEPC with R_{cp}=1.0 and 1.1 reduced the violation rapidly. As for the feasible rate, DEEPC with R_{cp}=0.5, 0.6 and 0.7 reduced the feasible rate to 0 and failed to optimize the violation. DEEPC with R_{cp}=0.8 and 0.9 attained the feasible rate of about 0.6 and 0.8, respectively. DEEPC with R_{cp}=1.0 and 1.1 attained the feasible rate of 1.0.

Therefore, it is thought that DEEPC with R_{cp}=0.8 and 0.9 attained proper control of ρ and kept a proper feasible rate with balancing the optimization of the objective value and the constraint violation.

5.4 Pressure Vessel Design

The structure of a pressure vessel is shown Figure 8. A pressure vessel is a cylindrical vessel which is capped at both ends by hemispherical heads. The vessel is designed to minimize total cost including the cost of material, forming and welding [32].

There are 4 design variables: thickness of the shell $T_s(x_1)$, thickness of the head $T_h(x_2)$, inner radius $R(x_3)$, length of the cylindrical section of the vessel not including the head $L(x_4)$. T_s and T_h are integer multiples of 0.0625 inch, which are the available thickness of rolled steel plates, and R and L are continuous. The problem has 4 inequality constraints.

This problem can be defined as follows:

$$\text{Minimize } f(\boldsymbol{x}) = 0.6224 x_1 x_3 x_4 + 1.7781 x_2 x_3^2 + 3.1661 x_1^2 x_4 + 19.84 x_1^2 x_3$$
$$\text{Subject to } g_1(\boldsymbol{x}) = -x_1 + 0.0193 x_3 \leq 0,$$
$$g_2(\boldsymbol{x}) = -x_2 + 0.00954 x_3 \leq 0,$$
$$g_3(\boldsymbol{x}) = -\pi x_3^2 x_4 - 4\pi/3 x_3^3 + 1296000 \leq 0,$$
$$g_4(\boldsymbol{x}) = x_4 - 240 \leq 0,$$
$$x_1, x_2 = 0.0625 i, i \in \{1, 2, \cdots, 99\}, 10 \leq x_3, x_4 \leq 200.$$

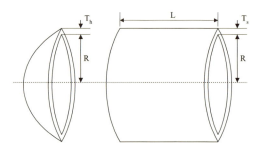

Figure 8. Pressure vessel design

This problem was solved by Sandgren [33] using Branch and Bound, by Kannan and Kramer [32] using an augmented Lagrangian Multiplier approach. Also, the problem was solved by Deb [34] using Genetic Adaptive Search (GeneAS) in the third category. In DEEPC, in order to solve this mixed integer problem, decision variables x_1' and x_2' are introduced instead of x_1 and x_2, and the values of x_1 and x_2 are given by the multiple of 0.0625 and the integer part of x'_1 and x'_2, respectively.

Experimental results on the problem are shown in Table 3. The good methods were DEEPC, MGA and Co-evolutionary penalty method. Note that MGA performed 50,000 FEs, Co-evolutionary penalty method performed 900,000 FEs, and other penalty based approaches performed 2,500,000 FEs.

Table 3. Results of pressure vessel design

Algorithm	FEs	Best	Average	Worst	S.D.
DEEPC	2,500	6250.7728	7966.0514	11035.4506	1009.6532
(R_{cp}=0.5)	5,000	6250.7728	7966.0514	11035.4506	1009.6532
	10,000	6250.7728	7966.0514	11035.4506	1009.6532
DEEPC	2,500	6076.6455	6649.9318	7769.0595	464.9608
(R_{cp}=0.6)	5,000	6076.6455	6649.9318	7769.0595	464.9608
	10,000	6076.6455	6649.9318	7769.0595	464.9608
DEEPC	2,500	6060.2313	6085.5033	6158.4623	24.3176
(R_{cp}=0.7)	5,000	6059.7144	6081.6473	6158.4623	26.6513
	10,000	**6059.7143**	6081.6461	6158.4623	26.6522
DEEPC	2,500	**6059.9256**	**6071.9757**	6155.0137	18.5594
(R_{cp}=0.8)	5,000	6059.7144	**6059.7155**	6059.7224	**0.0018**
	10,000	**6059.7143**	**6059.7143**	6059.7143	**0.0000**
DEEPC	2,500	6060.1098	6075.3990	6104.9839	13.0931
(R_{cp}=0.9)	5,000	6059.7144	6060.7438	6090.5268	5.5306
	10,000	**6059.7143**	6060.7414	6090.5262	5.5309
DEEPC	2,500	6060.3747	6082.2197	6155.5191	27.4325
(R_{cp}=1.0)	5,000	**6059.7143**	6061.7704	6090.5282	7.6856
	10,000	**6059.7143**	6061.7685	6090.5262	7.6858
DEEPC	2,500	6060.8312	6080.0938	6134.2962	17.5923
(R_{cp}=1.1)	5,000	6059.7144	6061.7699	6090.5278	7.6857
	10,000	**6059.7143**	6061.7685	6090.5262	7.6858
MGA	50,000	6069.3267	6263.7925	6403.4500	97.9445
Deb		6410.3811	N/A	N/A	N/A
Kannan		7198.0428	N/A	N/A	N/A
Sandgen		8129.1036	N/A	N/A	N/A
Co-evolutionary	900,000	6288.7445	6293.8432	6308.1497	7.4133
Static	2,500,000	6110.8117	6656.2616	7242.2035	320.8196
Dynamic	2,500,000	6213.6923	6691.5606	7445.6923	322.7647
Annealing	2,500,000	6127.4143	6660.8631	7380.4810	330.7516
Adaptive	2,500,000	6110.8117	6689.6049	7411.2532	330.4483
Death	2,500,000	6127.4143	6616.9333	7572.6591	358.8497

As for DEEPC, DEEPC with R_{cp}=0.8 attained the best average result of 6071.9757 in 2,500 FEs, the best average result of 6059.7155 in 5,000 FEs and the best average result of 6059.7143 in 10,000 FEs. It is thought that DEEPC with R_{cp}=0.8 is the best method in all settings of R_{cp}. Only in 2,500 FEs, DEEPC with R_{cp}=0.7, 0.8, 0.9, 1.0 and 1.1 can find better solutions on average than those of all other methods. DEEPCs except for R_{cp}=0.5 and 0.6 can find better solutions less than 1/20 FEs compared with other methods. So, DEEPC is the best method which can find very good solutions most efficiently and most stably.

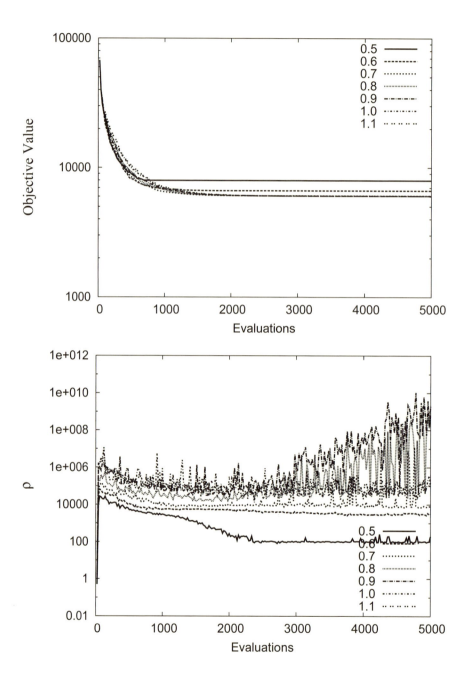

Figure 9. The graphs of the average values for the objective value and the penalty coefficient over the number of function evaluations in pressure vessel design problem.

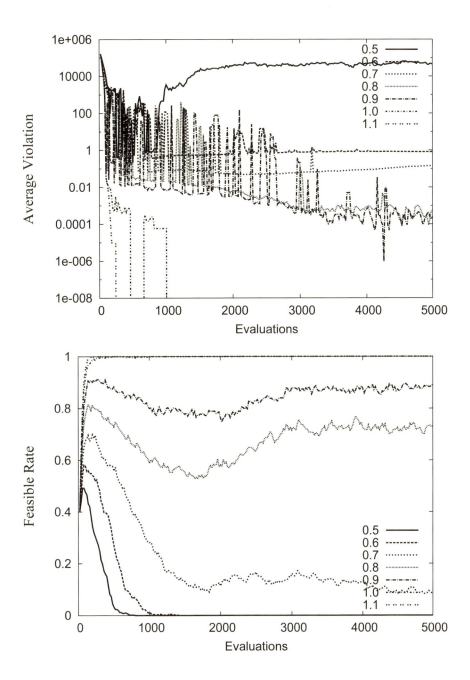

Figure 10. The graphs of the average values for the average constraint violation and the feasible rate over the number of function evaluations in pressure vessel design problem.

This problem is a difficult multi-modal problem. Other methods cannot find good solutions constantly even with 50,000 FEs. But DEEPC can find good solutions constantly only with 2,500 FEs. This result highlighted the robustness of DEEPC to multi-modal problems.

Figure 9 shows the graphs of the average values over 30 runs for the objective value of the best individual and ρ over the number of FEs obtained by DEEPC. Figure 10 shows the graphs of the average values over 30 runs for the average constraint violation in the population and the feasible rate.

As for the objective value, the value was converged to almost the same value except for DEEPC with R_{cp}=0.5, 0.6 and 0.7. As for the value of ρ, the value was increasing rapidly in an early stage and was decreasing gradually in DEEPC with R_{cp}=0.5, 0.6, 0.7 and 0.8, and was decreasing with large vibration in other settings of DEEPC. Larger R_{cp} tends to result in larger ρ.

As for the average violation, DEEPC with R_{cp}=0.5, 0.6 and 0.7 failed to reduce the violation, DEEPC with R_{cp}=0.8 and 0.9 reduced the violation gradually, and DEEPC with R_{cp}=1.0 and 1.1 reduced the violation rapidly. As for the feasible rate, DEEPC with R_{cp}=0.5 and 0.6 reduced the feasible rate to 0 and failed to optimize the violation. DEEPC with R_{cp}=0.7, 0.8 and 0.9 attained the feasible rate of about 0.1, 0.7 and 0.9, respectively. DEEPC with R_{cp}=1.0 and 1.1 attained the feasible rate of 1.0.

Therefore, it is thought that DEEPC with R_{cp}=0.8 and 0.9 attained proper control of ρ and kept a proper feasible rate with balancing the optimization of the objective value and the constraint violation.

6. Conclusions

In the penalty function method, feasible solutions can be found by increasing the penalty coefficient towards infinity theoretically, although it is difficult to do so computationally. In this study, the equivalent penalty coefficient value is proposed. Also, the adaptive control of the penalty coefficient based on the equivalent penalty coefficient values for POAs is proposed. The proposed method is introduced to DE and DEEPC is defined. Experiments for parameter settings were performed and it was shown that DEEPC could search for high quality solutions when the parameter R_{cp} was appropriate value. It was shown that DEEPC with R_{cp} in $[0.8, 1.1]$ could solve three benchmark problems very effectively and very stably compared with many other methods. Also, R_{cp} in $[0.6, 0.8]$ could realize smooth control of ρ.

In the future, we will apply DEEPC to various real world problems that have large numbers of decision variables and constraints. Also, we will introduce the idea of EPC to other POAs such as PSO.

Acknowledgment

This study is supported by JSPS KAKENHI Grant Numbers 26350443 and 17K00311.

References

[1] Michalewicz, Z., "A Survey of Constraint Handling Techniques in Evolutionary Computation Methods," *Proc. of the 4th Annual Conference on Evolutionary Programming*, Cambridge, Massachusetts: The MIT Press, pp. 135–155 (1995).

[2] Coello, C. A. C., "Theoretical and Numerical Constraint-Handling Techniques used with Evolutionary Algorithms: A Survey of the State of the Art," *Computer Methods in Applied Mechanics and Engineering*, Vol. 191, No. 11-12, pp. 1245–1287 (2002).

[3] Takahama, T. and Sakai, S., "Constrained Optimization by Applying the α Constrained Method to the Nonlinear Simplex Method with Mutations," *IEEE Trans. on Evolutionary Computation*, Vol. 9, No. 5, pp. 437–451 (2005).

[4] Coath, G. and Halgamuge, S. K., "A Comparison of Constraint-handling Methods for the Application of Particle Swarm Optimization to Constrained Nonlinear Optimization Problems," *Proc. of the 2003 IEEE Congress on Evolutionary Computation*, Canberra, Australia (2003), pp. 2419–2425.

[5] Homaifar, A., Lai, S. H. Y. and Qi, X., "Constrained Optimization Via Genetic Algorithms," *Simulation*, Vol. 62, No. 4, pp. 242–254 (1994).

[6] Joines, J. and Houck, C., "On the Use of Non-Stationary Penalty Functions to Solve Nonlinear Constrained Optimization Problems with GAs," Fogel, D. (ed.), *Proc. of the first IEEE Conference on Evolutionary Computation*, Orlando, Florida: IEEE Press (1994), pp. 579–584.

[7] Michalewicz, Z. and Attia, N., "Evolutionary Optimization of Constrained Problems," Sebald, A. and Fogel, L. (eds.), *Proc. of the 3rd Annual Conference on Evolutionary Programming*, River Edge, NJ: World Scientific Publishing (1994), pp. 98–108.

[8] Coello, C. A. C., "Use of a Self-adaptive Penalty Approach for Engineering Optimization Problems," *Computers in Industry*, Vol. 41, No. 2, pp. 113–127 (2000).

[9] Tessema, B. and Yen, G., "A Self Adaptive Penalty Function Based Algorithm for Constrained Optimization," Yen, G. G., Lucas, S. M., Fogel, G., Kendall, G., Salomon, R., Zhang, B.-T., Coello, C. A. C. and Runarsson, T. P. (eds.), *Proceedings of the 2006 IEEE Congress on Evolutionary Computation*, Vancouver, BC, Canada: IEEE Press (2006), pp. 246–253.

[10] Wang, Y., Cai, Z., Xhau, Y. and Zeng, W., "An Adaptive Tradeoff Model for Constrained Evolutionary Computation," *IEEE Trans. on Evolutionary Computation*, Vol. 12, No. 1, pp. 80–92 (2008).

[11] Deb, K., "An Efficient Constraint Handling Method for Genetic Algorithms," *Computer Methods in Applied Mechanics and Engineering*, Vol. 186, No. 2/4, pp. 311–338 (2000).

[12] Takahama, T. and Sakai, S., "Tuning Fuzzy Control Rules by the α Constrained Method which Solves Constrained Nonlinear Optimization Problems," *Electronics and Communications in Japan, Part 3: Fundamental Electronic Science*, Vol. 83, No. 9, pp. 1–12 (2000).

[13] Takahama, T. and Sakai, S., "Constrained Optimization by ε Constrained Particle Swarm Optimizer with ε-level Control," *Proc. of the 4th IEEE International Workshop on Soft Computing as Transdisciplinary Science and Technology (WSTST'05)* (2005), pp. 1019–1029.

[14] Runarsson, T. P. and Yao, X., "Stochastic Ranking for Constrained Evolutionary Optimization," *IEEE Trans. on Evolutionary Computation*, Vol. 4, No. 3, pp. 284–294 (2000).

[15] Mezura-Montes, E. and Coello, C. A. C., "A Simple Multimembered Evolution Strategy to Solve Constrained Optimization Problems," *IEEE Trans. on Evolutionary Computation*, Vol. 9, No. 1, pp. 1–17 (2005).

[16] Venkatraman, S. and Yen, G. G., "A Generic Framework for Constrained Optimization Using Genetic Algorithms," *IEEE Trans. on Evolutionary Computation*, Vol. 9, No. 4, pp. 424–435 (2005).

[17] Camponogara, E. and Talukdar, S. N., "A Genetic Algorithm for Constrained and Multiobjective Optimization," Alander, J. T. (ed.), *3rd Nordic Workshop on Genetic Algorithms and Their Applications (3NWGA)*, Vaasa, Finland: University of Vaasa (1997), pp. 49–62.

[18] Surry, P. D. and Radcliffe, N. J., "The COMOGA Method: Constrained Optimisation by Multiobjective Genetic Algorithms," *Control and Cybernetics*, Vol. 26, No. 3, pp. 391–412 (1997).

[19] Coello, C. A. C., "Constraint-handling Using an Evolutionary Multiobjective Optimization Technique," *Civil Engineering and Environmental Systems*, Vol. 17, pp. 319–346 (2000).

[20] Ray, T., Liew, K. M. and Saini, P., "An Intelligent Information Sharing Strategy within a Swarm for Unconstrained and Constrained Optimization Problems," *Soft Computing – A Fusion of Foundations, Methodologies and Applications*, Vol. 6, No. 1, pp. 38–44 (2002).

[21] Runarsson, T. P. and Yao, X., "Evolutionary Search and Constraint Violations," *Proc. of the 2003 Congress on Evolutionary Computation*, Piscataway, New Jersey: IEEE Service Center (2003), Vol. 2, pp. 1414–1419.

[22] Aguirre, A. H., Rionda, S. B., Coello, C. A. C., Lizárraga, G. L. and Montes, E. M., "Handling Constraints using Multiobjective Optimization Concepts," *International Journal for Numerical Methods in Engineering*, Vol. 59, No. 15, pp. 1989–2017 (2004).

[23] Wang, Y., Cai, Z., Cuo, G. and Zhou, Z., "Multiobjective Optimization and Hybrid Evolutionary Algorithm to Solve Constrained Optimization Problems," *IEEE Trans. on Systems, Man and Cybernetics, Part B*, Vol. 37, No. 3, pp. 560–575 (2007).

[24] Mallipeddi, R. and Suganthan, P. N., "Ensemble of Constraint Handling Techniques," *IEEE Transactions on Evolutionary Computation*, pp. 561–579 (2010).

[25] Storn, R. and Price, K., "Minimizing the Real Functions of the ICEC'96 Contest by Differential Evolution," *Proc. of the International Conference on Evolutionary Computation* (1996), pp. 842–844.

[26] Storn, R. and Price, K., "Differential Evolution – A Simple and Efficient Heuristic for Global Optimization over Continuous Spaces," *Journal of Global Optimization*, Vol. 11, pp. 341–359 (1997).

[27] Chakraborty, U. K. (ed.), *Advances in Differential Evolution,* Springer (2008).

[28] Hmmelblau, D., *Applied Nonlinear Programming*, New York: McGraw-Hill (1972).

[29] Gen, M. and Cheng, R., *Genetic Algorithms & Engineering Design*, New York: Wiley (1997).

[30] Hadj-Alouane, A. B. and Bean, J. C., "A Genetic Algorithm for the Multiple-choice Integer Program," *Operations Research*, Vol. 45, pp. 92–101 (1997).

[31] Rao, S. S., *Engineering Optimization*, New York: Wiley, third edn. (1996).

[32] Kannan, B. K. and Kramer, S. N., "An Augmented Lagrange Multiplier Based Method for Mixed Integer Discrete Continuous Optimization and Its Applications to Mechanical Design," *Journal of mechanical design, Trans. of the ASME*, Vol. 116, pp. 318–320 (1994).

[33] Sandgren, E., "Nonlinear Integer and Discrete Programming in Mechanical Design," *Proc. of the ASME Design Technology Conference*, Kissimine, Florida (1988), pp. 95–105.

[34] Deb, K., "GeneAS: A Robust Optimal Design Technique for Mechanical Component Design," Dasgupta, D. and Michalewicz, Z. (eds.), *Evolutionary Algorithms in Engineering Applications*, Berlin: Springer, pp. 497–514 (1997).

Contributors

Chris Czerkawski, *Professor, Hiroshima Shudo University*

Ph.D. in International Economics. Currently with Faculty of Economic Sciences, Hiroshima Shudo University. Previously teaching at Griffith University, Brisbane, Australia and Edith Cowan University in Perth, Australia. Research interests include foreign exchange markets, new financial markets in Asia Pacific area. Main teaching areas include International Finance, International Financial Management, International Economics.

Osamu KURIHARA, *Visiting Professor, Hiroshima University*

A visiting professor in Hiroshima University. He was educated at Meiji Gakuin University, Hiroshima University and Hiroshima Shudo University where he completed his Ph.D. He was a professor at the Faculty of Contemporary Sociology in Hiroshima Kokusai-Gakuin University from 2006 to 2016. He mainly lectures Macroeconomics and International Economics in several Universities. His research interests are Balance of Payments, Exchange rates and capital flows, currently and historically. He has been a director in Japan Academy for International Trade and Business from 2009.

Nan Zhang, *Professor, Hiroshima Shudo University*

Dr. Zhang is a professor of statistics in the Faculty of Economic Sciences, Hiroshima Shudo University, Japan. He came to Japan as a graduate research associate in 1989, studied in the Institute of Economic Research at Kyoto University, and received Ph.D. degree in 1993 from Ritsumeikan University, Japan. From April 1995 to March 1997, he worked as an associate professor at the Faculty of Commercial Sciences, Hiroshima Shudo University, Japan. In April 1997, he obtained professorship at the Faculty of Economic Science, Hiroshima Shudo University, Japan. He was a Visiting Scholar in East Asian Institute at Columbia University in the city of New York from 2001 until 2002. He also as a Visiting Scholar has ever worked in the Department of Statistics at University of California, Berkeley from 2007 to 2008, and the Department of Statistics at Stanford University from 2014 to 2015. His research focuses on Global Flow of Funds Analysis, Financial Econometrics, Economic Statistics and Monetary & Financial Statistics. Professor Zhang is a special research fellow of the Research Center for

Finance and Securities at Peking University, and he also is a consulting fellow of the Research and Statistics Department of the People's Bank of China. In 2008, he was named Technical Assistance Expert of the Statistics Department of the IMF. At Hiroshima Shudo University he teaches Statistics, Economic Statistics, and Financial Econometrics. He is a member of the Japan Statistical Society, Japan Society of Economic Statistics, Japan Society of Monetary Economics, the Japan Society of International Economics, the International Association for Research in Income and Wealth, and the International Association for Official Statistics.

Li Zhu, *Ph.D. Candidate, School of Statistics, Southwestern University of Finance and Economics, China.*

She received her Master Degree in 2010 from School of Statistics, Southwestern University of Finance and Economics. She was a researcher of Sichuan Provincial Statistical Science Research Institute from 2010 to 2018. Now, she is a Ph.D. Candidate, School of Statistics, Southwestern University of Finance and Economics and a fellowship of Graduate School of Economic Sciences, Hiroshima Shudo University, Japan until March 2019.Her research focuses on Economic Statistics and Econometrics.

Sithanonxay Suvannaphakdy, *Laos-Australia Development Learning Facility*

He received his Master Degree in 2010 and Ph. D. in Economics in 2013 from Graduate School of Economic Sciences of Hiroshima Shudo University. After completing his Ph. D., he worked at Asian Development Bank Headquarter as an economist and at Ministry of Industry and Commerce (Laos) as a national trade facilitation specialist. Since 2016, he is a researcher at Laos-Australia Development Learning Facility in Vientiane Capital, Lao PDR. He has published several papers in such international journals as Journal of Economic Development, Journal of Economic Development and Applied Econometrics, Journal of Southeast Asian Economies, and Asia-Pacific Economic Literature.

Toshihisa TOYODA, *Professor Emeritus, Hiroshima Shudo University*

He got his Ph. D. in Economics from Carnegie-Mellon University in 1971. He worked at Kobe University for 1966-2003 and at Hiroshima Shudo University for 2004-2012. He is now Project Professor at Center for Social Systems Innovation of Kobe University. His research interests include Macroeconomics, Development Economics, Applied Economics, and Economics of Natural Disasters. He has published many papers in such international journals as Econometrica, Journal of Econometrics,

Review of Economics and Statistics, Journal of Political Economy, International Economic Review, Journal of Economic Development, Asian Economic Journal, Empirical Economics, et ct.

Hiroyuki DEKIHARA, *Associate Professor, Hiroshima Shudo University*

Hiroyuki Dekihara is an associate professor at the Faculty of Economic Sciences in Hiroshima Shudo University, where he has been since 2017. He received his Ph.D. in Information Engineering from Hiroshima City University, Japan, in 2003. From 2001 to 2016, he worked at Hiroshima International University, eventually as an associate professor. His research interests span both C/S systems and data engineering. Much of his work has been on improving and developing mechanism of server that manages clients. He presented at a paper titled "An Extended Technique for R-tree to Manage Multiple Type Objects", Journal of Computational Methods in Sciences and Engineering, Vol.12, pp.S53-S61(2012). Currently, he is a member of research project developing educational frameworks and contents on key technologies of Forth Industrial Revolution: AI, IoT, Virtualization, etc.

Setsuko SAKAI, *Professor, Hiroshima Shudo University*

Setsuko Sakai graduated from the Faculty of Education, Fukui University, 1979. She finished her doctoral course of Informatics and Mathematical Science at Osaka University in 1984. She became a lecturer at the College of Business Administration and Information Science, Koshien University, in 1986, and then an associate professor of the Faculty of Education, Fukui University, in 1990. Since 1998, she has been with the Faculty of Commercial Sciences of Hiroshima Shudo University, where she is a professor in the Department of Business Administration. She is currently working on game theory, decision making, nonlinear optimization by using direct search methods, evolutionary computation, swarm intelligence and fuzzy mathematical programming. She is a member of the Operations Research Society of Japan, Japan Society for Fuzzy Theory and Intelligent Informatics, and the Japan Society for Production Management. She holds a D. Eng. degree. She has published papers such as "Tuning fuzzy control rules by α constrained method which solves constrained nonlinear optimization problems"(1999) and "Reducing the Number of Function Evaluations in Differential Evolution by Estimated Comparison Method using an Approximation Model with Low Accuracy"(2008) in The Transactions of the Institute of Electronics, Information and Communication Engineers, "Fast and Stable Constrained Optimization by the ε Constrained Differential Evolution", in Pacific Journal of Optimization (2009) and so on. She has also published papers in such journals as IEEE Transactions on Evolutionary Computation, Journal of Optimization Theory and its Applications, Transactions of the Japanese Society for Artificial Intelligence etc.

Tetsuyuki TAKAHAMA, *Professor, Hiroshima City University*

Tetsuyuki Takahama graduated from the Department of Electrical Engineering II, Kyoto University, in 1982. He finished his doctoral course in 1987. He became an assistant professor, and then a lecturer, at Fukui University in 1994. Since 1998, he has been with the Faculty of Information Science of Hiroshima City University, where he is an associate professor in the Department of Intelligent Systems. He is currently working on natural computing including evolutionary computation and swarm intelligence, nonlinear optimization and machine learning. He is a member of the Information Processing Society of Japan, the Japan Society for Artificial Intelligence, the Japanese Society of Information and Systems in Education, the Association for Natural Language Processing and IEEE. He holds a D. Eng. degree. He has published papers such as "Structural Optimization by Genetic Algorithm with Degeneration (GA^d)", in The Transactions of the Institute of Electronics, Information and Communication Engineers (2003), "Constrained Optimization by Applying the α Constrained Method to the Nonlinear Simplex Method with Mutations", in IEEE Transactions on Evolutionary Computation (2005), "Efficient Constrained Optimization by the ε Constrained Differential Evolution Using an Approximation Model with Low Accuracy", in Transactions of the Japanese Society for Artificial Intelligence (2009) and so on. He has also published papers in such journals as Information Processing Society of Japan Journal, International Journal of Innovative Computing, Information and Control Journal of Japan Society for Fuzzy Theory and Systems etc.

Series of Monographs of Contemporary Social Systems Solutions
Produced by
the Faculty of Economic Sciences, Hiroshima Shudo University

190 × 265 mm   5,000 yen (tax not included)

Volume 1   Social Systems Solutions by Legal Informatics, Economic Sciences and Computer Sciences

Edited by Munenori Kitahara and Kazunori Morioka   160 pages   ISBN 978-4-7985-0011-9

Preface
Chapter 1   The Concept of Personal Data Protection in Information Society ⋯ *Munenori Kitahara*
Chapter 2   On the Evaluation System of Public Sector ⋯ *Kazunori Morioka*
Chapter 3   Effects of Property Right Restriction: An Analysis Using a Product Differentiation Model ⋯ *Koshiro Ota*
Chapter 4   Tax Coordination between Asymmetric Regions in a Repeated Game Setting ⋯ *Chikara Yamaguchi*
Chapter 5   The Household Production and Comsumer Behavior ⋯ *Hiroaki Teramoto*
Chapter 6   Modeling a Sequencing Problem for a Mixed-model Assembly Line ⋯ *Shusaku Hiraki, Hugejile and Zhuqi Xu*
Chapter 7   Long-run Superneutrality of Money in Japanese Economy ⋯ *Md. Jahanur Rahman*
Chapter 8   A Parametric Study on Estimated Comparison in Differential Evolution with Rough Approximation Model ⋯ *Setsuko Sakai and Tetsuyuki Takahama*
Chapter 9   Fantappié Transformations of Analytic Functionals on the Truncated Complex Sphere ⋯ *Ryoko Wada*

Volume 2   The New Viewpoints and New Solutions of Economic Sciences in the Information Society

Edited by Shusaku Hiraki and Nan Zhang   160 pages   ISBN 978-4-7985-0055-3

Preface
Chapter 1   Economic Evaluation of the Recovery Process from a Great Disaster in Japan: The Case of Hanshin-Awaji Earthquake ⋯ *Toshihisa Toyoda*
Chapter 2   The Economic Analysis of Altruistic Consumer Behavior ⋯ *Hiroaki Teramoto*
Chapter 3   External Debt Default and Renegotiation Economics ⋯ *Chris Czerkawski*
Chapter 4   Statistical Observations on the External Flow of Funds between China and the U.S. ⋯ *Nan Zhang*
Chapter 5   Trade Flows in ASEAN plus Alpha ⋯ *Sithanonxay Suvannaphakdy and Toshihisa Toyoda*
Chapter 6   Inventory Policies Under Time-varying Demand ⋯ *Michinori Sakaguchi*
Chapter 7   RIDE: Differential Evolution with a Rotation-Invariant Crossover Operation for Nonlinear Optimization ⋯ *Setsuko Sakai and Tetsuyuki Takahama*
Chapter 8   The Network of Information Society Law ⋯ *Munenori Kitahara*
Chapter 9   The Function of the Copyright Mechanism: The Coordination of Interests of an Inventor and an Improver ⋯ *Koshiro Ota*

Volume 3 Social Systems Solutions Applied by Economic Sciences and Mathematical Solutions

Edited by Minenori Kitahara and Chris Czerkawski   156 pages ISBN 978-4-7985-0078-2

Preface

Chapter 1 The Collaboration of Law and InformationTechnology ··· *Munenori Kitahara*

Chapter 2 The Australian Broadband Policy: Theory and Reality ··· *Koshiro Ota*

Chapter 3 Evaluating the Impact of Mining Foreign Capital Inflows on the Lao Economy
··· *Phouphet Kyophilavong and Toshihisa Toyoda*

Chapter 4 Empirical Study of the Impact of the Thai Economy on the Lao Electricity Export
··· *Thongphet Lamphayphan, Chris Czerkawski and Toshihisa Toyoda*

Chapter 5 Calculating CO_2 Emissions for Coastal Shipping of Finished Cars by Pure Car Carriers in Japan   ··· *Min Zhang, Shusaku Hiraki and Yoshiaki Ishihara*

Chapter 6 A Statistical Model for Global-Flow-of-Funds Analysis ··· *Nan Zhang*

Chapter 7 The Reproducing Kernels of the Space of Harmonic Polynomials ··· *Ryoko Wada*

Chapter 8 A Comparative Study on Neighborhood Structures for Speciation in Species-Based Differential Evolution   ··· *Setsuko Sakai and Tetsuyuki Takahama*

Volume 4 Social Systems Solutions through Economic Sciences

Edited by Munenori Kitahara and Chris Czerkawski   156 pages ISBN 978-4-7985-0097-3

Preface

Chapter 1 Law and Technology: Privacy Protection through Technology ··· *Munenori Kitahara*

Chapter 2 The Signaling Role of Promotions in Japan ··· *Kazuaki Okamura*
—A Pseud-Panel Data Analysis

Chapter 3 The Chinese Spring Festival Model's Design and Application
··· *Gang Shi and Nan Zhang*

Chapter 4 Money and Real Output in Laos: An Econometric Analysis
··· *Inthiphone Xaiyavong and Chris Czerkawski*

Chapter 5 Literature Review on Ship Scheduling and Routing
··· *Min Zhang, Shusaku Hiraki and Yoshiaki Ishihara*

Chapter 6 Optimal Ordering Policies in a Multi-item Inventory Model
··· *Michinori Sakaguchi and Masanori Kodama*

Chapter 7 A Comparative Study on Graph-Based Speciation Methods for Species-Based Differential Evolution   ··· *Setsuko Sakai and Tetsuyuki Takahama*

Chapter 8 Sino-Japanese Compounds ··· *Paul Jensen*

Volume 5 Legal Informatics, Economic Science and Mathematical Research

Edited by Munenori Kitahara and Chris Czerkawski   104 pages ISBN 978-4-7985-0125-3

Preface

Chapter 1 Legal Justice through the Fusion of Law and Information Technology
···*Munenori Kitahara*

Chapter 2   The Role of International Transportation in Trade and the Environment
⋯Takeshi Ogawa

Chapter 3   A Comparative Study on Estimation Methods of Landscape Modality for Evolutionary Algorithms   ⋯Setsuko Sakai and Tetsuyuki Takahama

Chapter 4   Some Properties of Harmonic Polynomials in the Case of $\mathfrak{so}\,(p, 2)$
⋯Ryoko Wada and Yoshio Agaoka

Volume 6   New Solutions in Legal Informatics, Economic Sciences and Mathematics

Edited by Munenori Kitahara and Kazuaki Okamura   160 pages   ISBN 978-4-7985-0152-9

Preface

Chapter 1   Legality and Compliance through Deploying Information Technology
⋯Munenori Kitahara

Chapter 2   Three-Good Ricardian Model with Joint Production: A Schematic Reconsideration
⋯Takeshi Ogawa

Chapter 3   An Application of Cellular Automata to the Oligopolistic Market   ⋯Kouhei Iyori

Chapter 4   Development of a Multi-Country Multi-Sectoral Model in International Dollars
⋯Takashi Yano and Hiroyuki Kosaka

Chapter 5   Stochastic Inventory Model with Time-Varying Demand
⋯Michinori Sakaguchi and Masanori Kodama

Chapter 6   A Study on Adaptive Parameter Control for Interactive Differential Evolution Using Pairwise Comparison   ⋯Setsuko Sakai and Tetsuyuki Takahama

Chapter 7   On Some Properties of Harmonic Polynomials in the Case of $\mathfrak{so}\,(p, 2)$: Irreducible Decomposition and Integral Formulas   ⋯Ryoko Wada and Yoshio Agaoka

Volume 7   Contemporary Works in Economic Sciences: Legal Informatics, Economics, OR and Mathematics

Edited by Munenori Kitahara and Hiroaki Teramoto   130 pages   ISBN 978-4-7985-0179-6

Preface

Chapter 1   Audit and Compliance through Proactive Engineering Method   ⋯Munenori Kitahara

Chapter 2   Some Notes on Macroeconomic Policies: Abenomics in Japan
⋯Chris Czerkawski and Osamu Kurihara

Chapter 3   Health and Consumer Behavior   ⋯Hiroaki Teramoto

Chapter 4   Measuring Global Flow of Funds: Theoretical Framework, Data Sources and Approaches   ⋯Nan Zhang

Chapter 5   A Comparative Study on Detecting Ridge Structure for Population-Based Optimization Algorithms   ⋯Setsuko Sakai and Tetsuyuki Takahama

Chapter 6   Explicit Irreducible Decomposition of Harmonic Polynomials in the Case of $\mathfrak{so}\,(p, 2)$ ⋯Ryoko Wada and Yoshio Agaoka

**Volume 8 Challenging Researches in Economic Sciences:
Legal Informatics, Environmental Economics, Economics,
OR and Mathematics**
Edited by Munenori Kitahara and Hiroaki Teramoto   152 pages   ISBN 978-4-7985-0206-9

Preface

Chapter 1   Economics of Personal Information: The Ownership and Propertyzation of PII
⋯*Munenori Kitahara*

Chapter 2   The Asian Infrastructure Investment Bank and Building up a New Parallel
International Financial System   ⋯*Chris Czerkawski and Osamu Kurihara*

Chapter 3   Application of Environmental Economic Evaluation to Forest Conservation
Policies in Sabah, Malaysia   ⋯*Hiroshi Hasegawa*

Chapter 4   A Comparative Study on Grouping Methods for an Adaptive
Differential Evolution   ⋯*Setsuko Sakai and Tetsuyuki Takahama*

Chapter 5   Generators of Irreducible Components of Harmonic Polynomials
in the Case of $\mathfrak{so}(d, 2)$ ⋯*Ryoko Wada and Yoshio Agaoka*

Chapter 6   The Solvable Models of Noncompact Real Grassmannians   ⋯*Akira Kubo*

**Volume 9 Recent Studies in Economic Sciences:
Information Systems, Project Managements, Economics,
OR and Mathematics**
Edited by Atsushi Kadoya and Hiroaki Teramoto   126 pages   ISBN 978-4-7985-0229-8

Preface

Chapter 1   Economic Wealth and Prosperity in Christianity and Buddhism
⋯*Chris Czerkawski and Osamu Kurihara*

Chapter 2   Development of an Algorithm for Monitoring Eye Movement
Using Wireless EEG Headset   ⋯*Hiroyuki Dekihara and Tatsuya Iwaki*

Chapter 3   Big Data Techniques for Measuring Global Flow of Funds   ⋯*Nan Zhang*

Chapter 4   Some Conjectures Concerning Irreducible Components
of Harmonic Polynomials in the Case of $\mathfrak{so}(d, 2)$ ⋯*Ryoko Wada and Yoshio Agaoka*

Chapter 5   A Study on Selecting an Oblique Coordinate System
for Rotation-Invariant Blend Crossover in a Real-Coded Genetic Algorithm
⋯*Setsuko Sakai and Tetsuyuki Takahama*

Chapter 6   A Review of the Literature on Relationship Banking and SMEs   ⋯*Yajing Liu*

Chapter 7   Considering the Personality Development of Project Managers:
Proposal of a PM Report Card   ⋯*Tatsuo Sato*